Fun and Games
Outdoors

JACK COX

Fun and Games Outdoors

Games . . . for the beach, the park and the garden;
for commons and wide open spaces. Games for
camping holidays, picnics and days out in the country;
games for all outdoor occasions and all seasons

A Piccolo Original

PAN BOOKS LONDON AND SYDNEY

First published 1971 by Pan Books Ltd,
Cavaye Place, London SW10 9PG
ISBN 0 330 02797 2
5th printing 1975
©John Roberts Cox 1971

Printed and bound in England by
Cox & Wyman Ltd, London, Reading and Fakenham

Contents

	Introduction	7
1	The Games Bag	9
2	Beach Games	13
3	Games for Parks and Gardens	33
4	Games of Strength	61
5	Circle Games	71
6	Ball Games	81
7	Tag Games, Blindfold Games and Relay Races	95
8	Observation Games	107
9	Games for Younger Brothers and Sisters	113
	Index	123

Introduction

This book is intended to help any family or group of boys and girls to obtain fun and pleasure from simple games. It will give you lots of ideas for what to do in odd moments on holiday . . . by the sea, camping, on a farm, or simply on an outing to your nearest common or park – in fact, anywhere where you have to make your own fun and enjoyment. Most of the games in this book are for just a few players but I have included some team games for those occasions when you have friends to entertain and there are plenty of you. All the games have been tried and tested and there is endless scope for adding to them, adapting them to local conditions and improving them wherever the reader thinks this is necessary! What matters in the end is whether you enjoy yourself or not. So there are really no hard and fast rules about impromptu outdoor games.

I have indicated when necessary the suggested number of players for each game and, with the help of the index, a game for the needs of the moment can easily be found.

Jack Cox

1 THE GAMES BAG

Simple equipment is needed for outdoor fun and games. There are well-known outdoor games which you can buy at any good sports or toy shop, such as Jokari, but most of the outdoor games recommended in this book are based on simple equipment which can be found in any home.

It is a good idea to keep a strong bag or grip of some kind for your outdoor-games gear. Something which can easily be put in the boot of a family car (half the families of Britain had cars in 1970!) or perhaps something a little smaller for those who for one reason or another do not have cars but still enjoy a day's outing, picnics, and an afternoon in the nearest park or common.

For the car boot, an old canvas cricket bag or an ordinary holdall are both suitable. Whichever you choose, your games

9

bag should not be neglected when not in use. Do not leave it in the boot, as it will deteriorate in wet weather; keep it in any dry place indoors until needed – a coat cupboard, the hall cupboard under the stairs, anywhere like that, so long as it is dry.

To avoid mildew the gear in the bag should, ideally, be dried after a day out, and certainly after a holiday by the sea. Although the equipment collected may well be old it should not be so old that you have splinters on a cricket stump, for instance. Anything with a sharp or spiky point needs to be covered or protected in some way if it is not to pierce the bag. Like all sports bags the games bag will benefit from a good brushing occasionally, and hanging on the clothes-line in the sun to air.

Tie a name-and-address tag on the bag handle with your telephone number in case it ever gets lost, or your holiday address if you are going away. I well remember a family going by train to North Wales from Cheshire one year. They had to change at Crewe and popped into a refreshment room for a short while. Their games bag disappeared in that time and was sent off in error to Devon. But three days later it was back in North Wales, thanks to the tag.

Anything that rattles, such as cricket stumps or tent-pegs, needs tough elastic bands to be held firm with. A useful extra is a toilet bag with a sponge or damp face flannel in it, and a small rough hand towel. It freshens you up amazingly for the return journey home.

Here's my list of contents for the games bag, and you can add anything else you like for your own favourite games:

Old tennis balls (about six, if possible). Sorbo balls are needed for some games in preference to tennis balls. You could have a minimum of three each.

A plastic or lightweight football or suitable rubber ball.

Cricket ball (one or two).

Table-tennis balls (six in a cardboard box).

Old golf balls (at least six).

Rugby or soccer outer leather case, stuffed with an old towel.

A small rugby ball (useful alternative to football).

Beach ball.

A few lengths of rope with the ends whipped or bound with adhesive tape to stop fraying. They should be about 6 feet long.

A few wooden and metal tent-pegs, assorted sizes.

A pointed wooden dibber about 2 feet long for marking out games areas, squares, circles, etc, on sand.

Plastic white clothes-line for making quick circles on grass. One or two circles of varying size could be made up in advance from such a line and kept for future use.

A supply of rubber rings (hoop-la style).

Two or three deck quoits.

A boy's size cricket bat.

Notebook, scribbling block, pencils.

Two packs of playing cards in case it rains.

Two or three bean bags.

Small first-aid kit for the odd scratch, scrape, or bruise.

2 BEACH GAMES

Sand Castles

The most obvious game with sand castles is to see who can build the best one, but for this you need an impartial judge. Try a high sand castle contest: who can build the highest in a set time? No stones or other materials to be used.

A spiral sand castle is fun for young children. Make a fairly big mound of damp sand and then smooth a pathway round it from the top to the bottom in a spiral path. By rubbing a golf ball down the path, a shallow groove can be worn down which the ball will roll. If you can find a really round pebble, this will serve well as a ball. Take it in turns to see who can roll their ball down the path and farthest along the beach. Or dig several small holes in the beach and give points for each – highest points for the hole farthest from the path – and see who can gain the most points when rolling the ball down.

Sand Castles (also called Tailor's Dummy)

A good game for three boys on a sandy beach or the dunes. For some reason it always goes down well on a very breezy day. Two boys stand opposite each other a good yard apart while the third stands between them with his arms at his sides and sideways to the other two. He has to hold himself as stiff and rigid as possible at all times, with his arms at his sides. This is essential.

Now one boy pushes him like a sack to the other and he returns the compliment. The push must always be a direct one so that the 'Sand Castle' – the boy in the middle – is in a direct line. It goes on for some time and it's fun for all three. Inevitably, one boy tires and the push fails. Then the boy whose push failed takes up the middle position. And so it goes on until all the 'Sand Castles' are down.

A bit too boisterous for some, but always enjoyable to watch!

Freeze

This game has also been called Statues but Freeze is much better. Any number of players jump and run about, try head-over-heels, handstands, cartwheels or anything they like. As soon as the leader shouts 'Freeze!' they have to stop whatever they are doing immediately and freeze. There is a prize of some kind for the boy or girl who has frozen in the most strikingly original position, and who can keep it up after he or she has been adjudged the winner by the rest. Do not have the winner first time out. There should be several Freezes before a winner is eventually declared. A good game for parks and grassy glades as well as beaches.

Hopscotch

This is a good game for the beach because it doesn't leave any unsightly chalk lines on the ground. There are several variations, some of which consist of kicking a stone between the squares with the hopping foot, but as this tends to rub out the lines of the hopscotch on a beach, the best game is this one:

Draw a rectangle in the sand large enough for about a dozen sections, 18 inches square, to be marked within it. These can either be side by side, making a long, thin game, or in block form. Each square is given a number; the best way to do this is to put the appropriate number of small stones in one corner of the square because drawn figures get kicked out very easily. Each player selects a small flat stone and takes it in turn to toss the stone into one of the squares. If the stone goes outside the boundary lines, or if it touches any line, that go is forfeited and the next player takes a turn.

If the stone lands cleanly within a square, the thrower hops through every other square to his stone, marks his initials in the square with a stick and hops back, once again in every square. If he touches any line on the way, he forfeits that go and rubs out his initials. The aim is to get one's initials into every square and a player should try to get his stone into the farthest square first because it is a foul to hop in any square containing the player's own initials, and that go is forfeited if he does so.

If a player is unlucky enough to throw his stone accidentally into the first one or two squares and puts his initials in them, he must hop cleanly over those squares to reach those at the rear.

Catch Stone

This is a good game for a beach where there are plenty of stones. It should be played facing the sea and close to the water's edge so that there is no danger of anyone being hit by a pebble. A saucer-shaped hole is scooped out of the sand and a thick stick about 15 inches long is stuck upright in it. The hole should be about 6 inches across. A stone about the size of a golf ball is balanced on the end of the stick and the players stand on a shooting line drawn about 5 or 6 yards away. Each player takes it in turn to throw any sized pebble and knock the stone off the stick; but a point can only be claimed if the stone does not drop into the saucer. This means that players must hit the stone and not the stick, otherwise the stone drops straight into the hole.

Magic Carpets

You can have a lot of fun on a dull, chilly day when the sea looks terribly uninviting and you're shivering. You need a small mat or beach towel, and ideally between three and six players. Simply put the mat on a piece of level ground. Then someone must time you with a watch and on the word 'Go!' you all try to step on the mat and stay there. It is perfectly in order to drag someone off, shove them off, pull them this way and that, and so on. The time-keeper shouts 'Time!' exactly one minute later. Anyone not on the mat is out but has two more chances to redeem himself or herself. The last person still 'in' at the end wins.

Beach Rounders

Beach Rounders is always great fun, but you do need at least ten players, five a side, to make it go with a zip, so it is a game for holiday friends to join in.

You need a square marked out with a dibber in the sand, say, 10 yards each side, or as you wish, according to the space available. Each base is marked by a circle at the corner of the square. The only gear you need is a tennis ball, or a sorbo ball if you prefer, and a 'bat', which can be fashioned from any suitable piece of wood or can be a small boy's size cricket bat.

Toss for batting or fielding. The bowler stands in the centre of the square, and aims rather than bowls at the first striker. We ought to call the bowler a pitcher! The striker must hit the ball in three go's or be out. If he hits, he must run at once from first base, where he takes the strike, to the second base. The fielding side have a boy or girl on each base and as many others as are available placed at back stop and elsewhere.

If the striker fails to make first base, ie, before the ball is returned to the fielder there and bounced on the base circle, he is out and the next striker comes in. But if his hit is a good one and he manages to run round four sides of the square he has scored a rounder. If the striker makes only one base, or two, or three, he must stay there and the next player comes in to bat. The first striker then runs each time the ball is hit and only remains 'in' if he reaches final or fourth base without being run out. A striker is always out if his hit is caught cleanly.

You could have a situation where there are four strikers on the bases and no one to come in. In that case the whole side is out if the boy or girl on first base fails to hit the ball in three go's.

In the end, the side with the biggest score of rounders wins. Don't slog, please. A fair whack of the ball every time, keen fielding, and sound catching will make this a good game for everybody. A collection all round and the top rounders scorer can make his or her own choice of prize later on . . .

Corko!

During the year, collect all the wine-bottle corks you can and keep them safely in a suitable tin box. They dry out into splendid little objects for use in many good games. At the seaside you will find many more at the high-tide mark, among the seaweed and odds and ends.

Corko! is an old favourite among Welsh boys who live by the sea. They play it simply by standing on a marked line and then placing a cork in the palm of their left hand, if they are right-handed. Then, using the thumb and second finger of the right hand, they flick the cork as far as they can. Away it goes like an arrow! Ping!

Each boy (or girl) has three corks and the winner is the one who can flick a cork the farthest distance. The winner can have an ice-cream, or the loser can pay a forfeit – put a couple of corks in each sandal or beach shoe and then walk round a marked circle in the sand. You look like Charlie Chaplin!

Bucket Corko

Try this variation of Corko! You play the same way except you have to flick the cork into a small cardboard box, sand bucket, or plastic kitchen bucket. The game goes on longer than Corko! because you only score a point if your cork goes in the bucket or box. So you could have a game among five or six boys and girls with, say, six flicks each or work it out according to your stock of corks. It's a very good game for a wet or dull day, when you can play under the trees or in a sheltered barn or boat-house until it fines up again.

Uncle Frank

This is an outdoor game to play on any hard, flat, sandy beach when the tide is out. It was immensely popular in my family when I was a boy and has stood the test of time over the years. My father would draw some large and amusing cartoons on the beach with a sharp-pointed stick, usually of some sporting or political personalities of the day, sometimes of us. But he left odd things off such as hands or feet, an odd leg, perhaps, sports gear, hats, spectacles, and so on. It was up to us to add these and it always gave us a lot of fun. Often other families would join in. My cousins called it Uncle Frank because that was my father's name.

If you can invent some game that brings fun and enjoyment to you and your friends on a summer holiday or a day by the sea, make sure you keep it going so that different generations can enjoy it in later years. That is how so many impromptu family games have developed into a tradition.

Fetch

A good game for a hot day – a quiet 'sitting-down' game. Choose a leader who sits in front of the rest of the players. *He must not say a single word.* The game begins when he raises one arm high. Off we go! He (or she) now has to mime somehow or describe by sign language only some article that he wants someone to get for him. It must, of course, be an article that is near at hand. The first person to produce *the right article* wins, and so on.

This game can be very funny. If you have seen the antics of someone trying to describe, say, a fish finger in sign language, or a sausage-shaped balloon, it is funny enough. When you see the things the players produce it can be even funnier.

In and Out

Many beaches have marvellous shallow pools left by the tide and you can have all kinds of games in swimming gear.

When the leader shouts 'In the pool!' everybody jumps in and stops dead. 'Out of the pool!' means you have to jump out again as quickly as possible, and then the leader really can get going. 'In' and 'Out' commands can follow as rapidly as possible. Naturally, he may shout three 'In's' or 'Out's' in succession which probably leads to at least one player falling headlong in the water! This could be the object of the exercise!

If he shouts 'In the sand!' or 'Over the water!' or any other nonsense command you have to ignore it if you can. It's a noisy, splashing game which children love on a summer's day. It can be quite hilarious if there is any slippery seaweed about.

Do make certain before you start that the pool really is shallow and that there are no sharp bits of rock or shell about.

Skimming

Boys and girls love to skim flat pieces of rock, stone or shell across the sea on a calm, still day so that they make two, three, four, or even more, skimming hits on the water before the objects disappear. The rock has to be really flat on both sides and skimming is a good test of throwing skill – a good cricket fielder is usually a dab hand at this.

For some reason dark-coloured stones are the best skimmers – probably because very flat, smooth white ones seem to be scarcer. Naturally, you always lose your stones. A good idea is to cut a dozen or more oval pieces of wood – which should not be too light in weight – of the size you can easily throw, say, about 3 inches long. Easily made at school, or in the garage or kitchen, with a fretsaw, these pieces of wood will skim even better than stones on a day when the sea is as calm as a mill pool. But instead of losing them you find that they float back to shore and you can collect all of them, or most of them, later. Paint them with a bold bright colour which will show up well on sand, such as bright orange, and they will stand out in the flotsam and jetsam when the tide comes in.

Beach Cricket

Beach cricket almost explains itself but be wary of one thing – the size of the beach and the extent of the outfield as a result! The slogger at beach cricket will spoil the game for everybody especially when he smites the ball into the ocean.

I suggest you mark out a fairly big circle of sorts, or perhaps an oval would be more appropriate for cricket, with your dibber. Let everybody have a good idea of where the circle or oval is.

On a family outing or picnic, or holiday by the sea, you won't have enough players for a proper game so let's imagine it's four or five boys and girls and two assorted dads. (The mums are sure to be talking when cricket is mentioned.)

Mark out a reasonably-sized pitch in the centre of your circle or oval and set up three stumps at each end in the usual way. No bails are necessary, of course, for a simple beach game. Play with a tennis ball and a boy's size bat which you can easily make yourself if you haven't got one.

Put all your names on pieces of paper in a sand bucket and draw lots for a batting order. Whoever is last in the batting order becomes first in the bowling order and he, or she, has a special allowance of twenty balls an over. (On no account write and tell the MCC.)

Off you go! The real thing is overarm deliveries and 'unders' for the young ones. The point is no one must hit the ball so hard that it goes outside the circle or oval. If so, they are jolly well *OUT*.

The idea is skilful placing of the ball so that it remains in the circle or oval just out of reach of fielders who must dash after it and try and get a batsman run out in the accepted way – except we have no bails in beach cricket, but a ball hitting a stump is enough.

In this way the game soon becomes fast and furious and you will soon attract boys and girls from other families on the beach who want to join in. Soon you might be able to set up a match, even if you only get six or seven a side.

In Beach Cricket a batsman cannot stonewall, or play good strokes and stay there all day. If he hits the ball, he is only allowed to stay in his crease without running three times in any one over of twenty balls. So for the most part he will be running like mad to score one or more runs while someone fields the ball and tries to get him run out. Of course, there are no boundaries.

No book-keeping either, please. It spoils holiday cricket. Let every batsman keep his or her own score. It will be mainly in singles and sooner or later he or she will be out by hitting the ball a bit too hard so that it zooms over the magic circle or oval you drew with the dibber.

Time for an ice-cream!

Beach Tennis

Beach Tennis is a good game at any time but is one of the very best for a rainy day. Then you only need wear your swimsuits or trunks and a pair of plimsolls (called pumps in the North) and you're all set. Make sure you get a brisk rub-down with a rough towel as soon as the game is over.

A good cheap substitute for a tennis net is a length of rot-proofed pea or bean netting with 3-inch square mesh. A 14-foot length 3 feet wide costs about 25 new pence and will give you lots of wear and tear.

To get the netting taut you will need two guylines on either end attached to the top of the net with some stout twine or sisal. Put a fixed loop on the end of each guyline – simply with some twine or a small metal curtain ring. Then the netting can be set up between two stakes with two guy-lines on each end pegged down in the sand or grass with wooden tent-pegs.

Play your beach tennis any way you like. Tennis balls and table-tennis bats are quite good and will give an impromptu but satisfying game at any time. I think it is best played with rubber quoits, the idea being that you have to throw your quoit over the net – your opponent drops a point if he fails to catch it.

Horseshoes

This game comes from South Africa where it is simply called Quoits but, to distinguish it from many other kinds of Quoits which cannot be played outdoors very easily, I call it Horseshoes.

First of all, you must get hold of a small, fairly thick pointed stake or stick. A 12-inch beech or oak wooden tent-peg would be ideal because it can be driven into the ground or sand easily without splitting. Put your stake or peg in so that about 6 inches is left sticking out of the ground or sand.

Now mark distances from the stake by drawing a straight line across the sand with your dibber, or by placing several 6-foot lengths of rope across in front of the stake. I suggest you make the distances from the stake at 3, 6, 9, 12 and 15 feet intervals. If you think this is too much or too little, adjust the distances accordingly.

The 'Quoits' can be real or imitation metal horseshoes but they are rather hard to find these days and are too heavy to carry around anyway. I suggest you make your own for this game from leather or plywood. Cut out the shape of a horse-shoe roughly and mark it out on a piece of plywood or hardboard, cutting it out with a fretsaw. You need at least six, and about ten is a good number to have in the games bag.

An alternative to plywood horseshoes is to use leather

ones. You can take the soles off discarded leather shoes and cut the middle part away so that you are left with the rough shape of a leather horseshoe. Or you could go to a shoe repairer and ask him to cut you some rough leather horseshoes from any spare bits he has available. Two pence each is a fair price, perhaps three pence for super ones.

Now stand behind the various lines working your way backwards from 3 to 15 feet. Let everyone have a go, trying to ring the stake in the ground with a horseshoe. It seems hard at first but you get very good at it before long.

Once you have all mastered the art of ringing the stake with a horseshoe, you can try various games of skill. The one I like best is to play this game on a stretch of hard, clean sand. Then you can draw several circles around your stake with the dibber at roughly 6-inch intervals, and mark them so that the thrower would gain so many points for each ring in which his quoit landed if he didn't score a bull. The circle nearest the quoit would count most and points would decrease outwards to the outer circle. You still stand 3, 6, 9, 12 or 15 feet back. It is an exciting and quite skilful game.

French Bowls

Wherever you go in France, and wherever French people go on holiday, you will see the traditional game of *Les Boules* (French Bowls) being played. It is also called *Pétanque*.

They play it endlessly at most times of the year in the boulevards and parks, on any stretch of suitable grass or sand and on every kind of beach. Basically, a small metal ball is thrown forward, say, 15 to 20 feet. This is the jack. Then each player in turn throws his ball – which is somewhat larger and may be metal, wooden or plastic – in an effort to hit the jack or get as near to it as he or she can.

There are many intricate ways of measuring the distance from the jack by individual throwers with pocket tape-measures and lengths of knotted string with the measure between knots being so many centimetres.

There is no need to do this for a family game although Mum might have a tape-measure with her if she is a knitter. Every boy and girl has a ready-made tape-measure with his or her hand. You should know what your span is from the tip of the thumb to the tip of your little finger when the hand is outstretched. It will change as you grow, so check it two or three times a year with a ruler. You also need to know the length of the top joint of your thumb, from the 'bend' to the top of the nail, which I think is the most useful rough measure of all. Another good measure is the width of your four fingers on either hand when the fingers are close together. Yet another is the distance from the tip of your thumb to the tip of your first finger when both are outstretched.

So you can easily measure distances of a ball from a jack, and so on. You don't need the real thing to play French Bowls though it is fun to play with those clanking little metal balls if you are on holiday in France or Spain. A good alternative is a cricket ball for the jack, and tennis balls for the individual throws. If the tennis balls are very lively on a dry warm day, soak them in a bucket of water for half an hour or so. I have seen the game played well on beaches which are unsuitable for many other games because of the rough nature of the pebbles, rock, and sand. Wooden balls were used, the jack being made of teak or some other heavy wood, in a school workshop, and the balls for throwing from beech.

French Bowls is a progressive game. You move on from the first throw along a stretch of beach or park and perhaps you will be 400 yards on after an hour, keeping a simple score card of the winner of each throw. I have seen French families bowling along a mile of Spanish beach, keeping it up for hours!

I think we'll say one hour before lunch or after tea when the mood takes us.

Brief Pause: Making a Bowl of Stones

This is *not* a game! Don't throw your collections of lovely beach stones and pebbles away. Take them home and wash and clean them thoroughly – using a nailbrush if necessary. Then buy the largest goldfish bowl you can, put the pebbles and stones in it, cover with clean water and stand in some place in the home where the sunlight will fall on it or through it. The bowl of stones will remind you of many happy picnics or days out or holidays at the seaside. All your family and friends will admire it, and may even copy the idea! You should change the water in the bowl, and perhaps the position of the stones and pebbles, about three times a year, or else a greeny growth will start forming on the stones.

When you wash them the stones will quickly clear of this growth if you put a little bleach in the water in which you clean them.

Another good idea is to colour the water slightly to remind you of the sea. If the sea at your holiday or picnic spot looked very blue, a few drops of blue ink can be added. If it was very green, then use green ink. You could also add a few drops of red ink to give you a pinky water for your pink or reddish stones. Your friends *might* believe you if you said you had a pink sea on the day you collected the stones!

If you have a pen friend or a relative in Australia or the West Indies, they might send you some coral and other wonderful stones to put in your bowl, if you ask them nicely.

So long as you have a Bowl of Stones in the house somewhere – perhaps in your own room if you are lucky enough to have one – you will be constantly reminded about getting outdoors for lots more fun – especially when the sun shines.

Jokari

One of the best of all beach games, especially if you enjoy tennis or squash. It seems to appeal to players of all ages, old and young alike, and both sexes, and gives excellent exercise in a confined space. I think it is best played so that one always serves the ball, which is on a long elastic cord attached to a small heavy box on the ground, into the prevailing wind. A great game for one or two players. It can be bought at any good toy shop or sports outfitters and will give years of fun if treated with reasonable care. The elastic cords can easily be replaced.

Beach Ball

A holiday by the sea would not be complete without a beach ball in the games bag. They vary in size. The plastic football-size can be used for all kinds of passing and punting games and is possibly best used if there is a wall, say, a harbour wall, or groyne, at low tide, in the vicinity. Then one, two, or three, players can invent their own games in which the ball is constantly tapped with the bare feet against the wall or groyne so that it goes to colleagues who will return the compliment. Variations include heading, tapping with the knee or elbow (but never the hand), and dribbling. Heading on its own makes a fine game and for sheer skill in this direction one has only to see three or four Spanish boys playing with one in the cool of a summer evening. It is a *crime*, they tell me, to let the ball 'hit the deck'. A beach ball must be kept in the air.

Large beach balls tend to be used for less skilful games but they are loved by small children for 'pushing' games in which they do nothing but try and push the ball forward with two hands over a line on the sand while their opponent does exactly the same in the opposite direction. Great fun in shallow pools, too.

Square Hop

Take two lengths of rope, each about 6 feet long, and lay them on the ground or sand, one crossing the other at right angles. If you wish, and the ground or sand is suitable, mark out the remaining sides of the square so that you have four check-board squares, each square having two sides bounded by ropes and two by marked lines.

Now label the squares clearly A, B, C, and D. This will be easy if you play Square Hop as a beach game. On grass you will have to memorize them.

One player now stands in one of the four squares and has to hop or jump to another square on the leader's command. If the player is in A and the leader shouts 'C', the player must hop or jump smartly to C, and so on. When a mistake is made the player concerned has to drop out and someone else takes over. The winner is the one who stays in the squares longest on a time check.

The leader tries to make the player do a wrong jump by calling out letters which are not A, B, C, or D, such as K, G, L, Z, etc. And he can be as quick as he likes in shouting the letters. So it all depends on concentration – knowing exactly where you are and where the other letters are in relation to your position. The player should always face the leader. This game can be fast and furious!

Time Hop

This game is very similar to Square Hop except that it takes place in a large circle drawn out in the sand or ground with the dibber. Instead of four squares we have a large circle divided into four segments by the same two ropes crossing at right angles. Instead of the letters A, B, C, and D we have the Time Zones of '1 o'clock – 2 o'clock – 3 o'clock' in the first zone. Moving clockwise we have 4, 5, and 6 o'clock in the second; 7, 8, and 9 o'clock in the third; and 10, 11, and 12 o'clock in the fourth.

The player stands in the first zone and faces the leader who shouts out a time, and at once the player must hop or jump into the right zone, or stay where he or she is. It is a bit harder than Square Hop because there are three times in each zone!

But the leader cannot fox you in Time Hop by shouting out a letter which is not on the squares – there are only twelve hours to remember. But be wary of 'midnight' or 'noon' or 'midday'. All are 12 o'clock. Again it's fast and furious fun.

The winner is the one who stays in the clock long enough without making a mistake which means someone must be clock-watching properly.

SPORTS DAY

When you go on holiday, especially at the seaside, you often meet families and get to know them. One of the joys of family holidays is simply meeting new friends. Quite often they become friends for life, just through a cheerful beach game on a sunny August morning!

One day your family and perhaps one or two others you have met on the beach can have a lot of fun with a 'Sports Day'. You need about a dozen people of all ages ready to make it a big success with an all-in picnic lunch to follow. But you can adapt it anyway you like and it can be fun if there are only four or five or six of you. Here goes . . .

Best time of the day is late morning on a day that's not too hot – perhaps a good deal of cloud about, or a stiff breeze to get everybody in the right mood. If it's one of those very hot, very still days, put it off until it's cooler and breezier.

Invent all your own sporting ideas! Here's some of mine but yours may be much better:

(1) **Chariot Race** round a set course on the beach. The chariot consists of two boys and a third with head down like a rugby scrum – then a jockey on his back, one of the lighter kind, please! Two or three chariots make a fine race so long as you take care not to make it too boisterous.

(2) **Throwing the Cricket Ball.** Easy! Longest throw wins. Have two classes, one for girls (all ages!) one for boys (all ages also). Fun.

(3) **Throwing a Football.** The ball could be a real football, a football bladder, a rugby ball, a case stuffed with towels or any other suitable beach ball. Again two classes for boys and

CHARIOT RACE

girls. The ball should be thrown with two hands from a standing position, as in soccer – and the winner might be a member of a girl's netball team at school. Good game this.

(4) **Throwing the Javelin.** The 'javelin' is nothing more than a long suitable rod made of wood – if you are holidaying on a farm there are sure to be lots of suitable rods about. Otherwise, try and borrow a broom handle, or a suitable garden tool or appliance that has seen its best days. I used a

long lightweight metal rod used for propping up rows of runner beans.

(5) **Throwing the Hammer.** The 'hammer' can be a very simple wooden makeshift, a *small* wooden tent mallet, or an Indian club – anything you have, in fact, so long as it isn't a real hammer or anything so heavy as to be dangerous. Longest throw wins, and make sure there is no one directly in the line of fire!

(6) **Hop, Skip and Jump.** This explains itself and is always a firm favourite. The girls *always* win! Try and have the final jump into a pit of soft, clean sand.

(7) **Long Jump.** Explains itself (or see page 56). Use the same setting as your Hop, Skip, and Jump event.

(8) **Water Relay.** Carry a bucket (seaside variety) of seawater round a convenient rock at the best possible speed without spilling any. At the end the team with the most water left wins.

(9) **Dads' Only Race.** Each dad has to carry a boy or girl in the fireman's lift hold over one shoulder round a convenient rock or bush and back.

(10) **Mums' Only Race.** The old egg-and-spoon routine except that the spoon is a wooden porridge spoon and the egg is a golf ball. Then it becomes quite a game of skill. Poor Mum! Tell her it's best in bare feet.

(11, 12, etc.) Events of your own choice. When this Sports Day is over and you've had a good picnic and a rest, spend the rest of the afternoon exploring the hidden mysteries of pools left by the tide, scrambling over seaweed and sand dunes and tufty marram grass. Best of all, learn something about boats.

Footnote: see Mini-Olympics (page 55) for a Sports Day more suited to a park, common, or large garden.

3 GAMES FOR PARKS AND GARDENS

Treasure Hunts
There can be many variations on this, from sticking pegs into a sand patch to a game that takes the players out into the woods and fields. The first is a garden or beach game and

is played on a patch about a yard square. One player buries the 'treasure', which can be anything from a cotton-reel to a sea shell, in the earth and smoothes the patch afterwards. The other players who, of course, have not seen this, then place a stone on the spot where they think the treasure is buried. Nearest to the actual place then becomes the burier.

To make the game a little more elaborate, a larger patch

is used and each player throws a dice and whatever number the dice shows, the player places that many stones.

Proper Treasure Hunts should take place over a wider area (eg, a park) and have clues. They can still be played in a garden but some preparation is needed out of sight of the players. The clues can be quite simple: 'The third rose bush from the front door' or 'Look behind the garden shed' but the places where they are hidden should preferably be out of sight of each other. For a number of players a Circular Hunt can be played. There is no actual treasure and the winner is the first one to find all the clues and finish the course. The advantage of this game is that all players can start off at the same time but all will be on different clues. Each clue leads on to the next one and the last leads back to the first. There should be a few more clues than there are players, to keep the game open, and players must replace clues exactly as they found them. Each player must be told where one clue is.

Full-scale Treasure Hunts can be played over a wide area and the clues can be made as simple or as elaborate as you wish. Some clues can be just drawings or photographs of the next point along the trail and the players have to identify it; others can be in the form of puzzles or codes, or a description of the place: 'Find where the silver birch tree has fallen across the stream' or, more puzzling, 'Horses couldn't tell the time here', which was an actual clue used in a Treasure Hunt and referred to a riding school where the clock on the house had been stopped for many years. Such Treasure Hunts will take a whole afternoon to play and can be combined with a picnic at a central point. A good idea is for each player to carry a set of Emergency Clues so that if he gets lost, or cannot work out the clue, he opens the envelope for that clue and it tells him where to go next, but he loses a certain number of points from his total score. The player with the most points remaining at the end of the game is the winner.

After all this activity, do make sure that there is a treasure of some kind at the end, or you will have some very disappointed players.

Nature Paintings

This can be a group activity, with all members painting the same picture, or individual pictures can be painted. It can be done in a garden but there is more chance of variety out in the country, on a picnic or holiday. The rough outline of a picture is sketched on a sheet of paper and this has to be coloured in, using only natural materials. The picture should have big and bold subjects – a mountain and lake scene, or fields and woods, and so on – and the colours can be found by rubbing various natural objects on the appropriate section of the picture. The aim is to *paint* a picture, not build it up. Suggested materials for colours include grass, which naturally gives green; various soils give different degrees of brown; flower petals will often render the same shades as the petals; berries can give many shades of red through to purple, and so on. An independent judge decides which picture is the best from the colours chosen, not how good the drawing is.

Nature Pictures

This is a three-dimensional style of the Nature Painting only this time a picture or scene is built up of natural materials. Once again, it can be a group project or individual, but what must be decided beforehand is whether a set subject is tackled or each player composes any scene he likes. A piece of cardboard or hardboard can be given to each player as a baseboard, or the scene can be set up directly on the ground. Suitable subjects could be 'The Teddy Bears' Picnic', or 'A Saxon Village', or even a more imaginative one such as 'Shipwrecked on a Desert Island', or 'Survivors of a crash on Mars'. Only natural materials may be used: pine cones, pebbles, leaves, grasses, pieces of wood, bark, twigs, berries, water, soil, and so on. There are enough natural items in any garden or park to make any number of Nature Pictures.

Orange Rolling
This needs at least four players divided into two groups but the more players there are, the better. Two parallel courses are marked out, not too long but they should run round

flowerbeds, between trees, and so on. Each group is given an orange which must be pushed round the course with noses only. One player from each group starts off and after a yard or so another player takes over, and so on until each player has had several pushes and the end of the course is reached. This can be played as a Parents v. Children race – with the children usually winning!

There are so many types of plastic bottle around today – liquid detergent, shampoo, cordial bottles, etc – that there must be hundreds of uses for them in games.

Skittles
This is an obvious one and for this game ten bottles, preferably all of the same type, should be a quarter filled with
water to give them stability. They should be stood in tri-
angular formation at one end of a suitable bowling area with
the single bottle nearest the bowler. Each player, using
tennis balls, has three bowls at the bottles and claims a point
for each bottle knocked down. An extra point is claimed if
all the bottles have been knocked down by the third bowl,
two points if all are down by the second bowl, and three
points if the first ball knocks them all down, so a player can
score a maximum of thirteen in any one round by knocking
down all the skittles with the first ball.

Bar Skittles
Usually this is an *indoor* skittle game with the skittles on a
square baseboard around a pole. On the top of the pole is
fastened a cord, and at the other end of the cord is a small
ball which the player swings and attempts to knock over the
skittles. The cord length is adjusted so that the ball barely
brushes the outermost skittle, and it takes a degree of skill to
knock it down. The same game can be adapted on a larger
scale for the garden. Plastic bottles are used and are grouped
on one side of a tree, washing-line post, or something erec-
ted for the game. The cord is fastened about 8 to 10 feet up
and a suitable weight tied to the far end. The weight can be
anything from a boxing-glove to a bundle of paper, but an
authentic touch is added if an old plastic model plane is
used. Players stand on the opposite side of the pole to the
skittles and swing the weight round to try and knock the
bottles over. Scoring is the same as for ordinary skittles.
The cord should be adjusted so that the weight just touches
the outside skittle. A player may hold the weight at any
height he likes but the cord must be taut before the weight
is released; a slack cord counts as a foul and that swing is
forfeited.

Squirters

Soft plastic detergent bottles are needed for this game – and all players must wear their swimming gear! A bucket of water is placed at one side of the games area and a circle about 4 feet in diameter drawn round it. Each player is given a detergent bottle, which must still have the nozzle attached, and at the starting signal they run to the bucket and draw as much water as possible into their bottle by compressing them and dipping the nozzle into the water. The aim is to try and squirt water over the backs of the other players, and not get squirted themselves, of course. When a bottle is empty a player may refill it at the bucket but no player may squirt water, or be squirted at, while in the circle. Any player who can prove his back is dry after, say, two minutes is the winner, although this is most unlikely!

Fill the Bucket

This can be played by individual players or by teams, depending upon how many buckets and bottles are available. Each player or team has an empty bucket at one end of the area and there is one bucket full of water at the other end; this bucket will serve for all players but it will need topping up quite a lot. Players run up to the bucket of water, draw in as much as they can into their plastic bottles and then run back and squirt it into their empty buckets. If it is a team game, the bottle is handed to the next player to fill; individual players just run up and down as many times as they can in a time limit of two minutes.

On the finishing signal, players must stop and no water is allowed to be put into their buckets. The water they have collected is then measured carefully and the winner declared. If all the competitors have buckets of exactly the same size, measurements can be taken by dipping a rule into the water, but if the containers vary then the water must be poured carefully into some form of measuring container, such as a graduated kitchen jug.

Courier

A simple game for a number of players, perhaps most suitable for the day you entertain your friends from the next village or town – when there are likely to be quite a number of boys and girls about, say five, six, or seven.

The players are stationed at various places a reasonable way apart – 50 yards is excellent if you can. One by a tree, one under a hedge or by a gate, and so on.

The leader repeats a message *slowly, and twice only*, to the first player who has to run like mad to the second player and repeat it to him or her, and so on to the last player. Then all run back to the leader to hear the last player's message and compare it with the original. Usually, it sends people into shrieks of laughter and you can try it again later on.

The classic howler for this game was once told by the late Lord Baden-Powell, founder of the Scout and Guide movements:

'Send reinforcements – the enemy is going to advance!' It ended up as 'Send three and fourpence – we are all going to a dance!'

My own favourite message comes from a notebook I kept when training boy cadets in the Royal Engineers at one stage in my life.

The message I gave to Cadet No 1 was: 'There are too many ships in the line. Tell two to retire. Sender O.L.'

It came back an hour later from Cadet No 10 who was some three miles distant: 'There are too many chips in mine. Two more for a tyre. Oh hell!'

I have a lot more gems but space is short. Have a go yourself.

Aeroplates (or Flying Saucers)

I used to love plate spinning when I was a boy and even when I grew up I still enjoyed it immensely. We used to hold an enamel camp plate in our hand like a discus, ie, in the palm of the hand, holding the plate from the bottom with the edge at right angles to the ground. Then with one mighty sweep we would hurl the plate away from us. Away it went like a bird, curling and skimming in the breeze, until it landed and bounced quite a long way off.

All very well and great fun! But far too many plates became dented, buckled or impossible to use as plates afterwards with all that chipped enamel. Try explaining that one to your mother when you get home!

And another thing. Spinning enamel plates can be *dangerous*. I've never seen it happen, but supposing one hit another boy or girl on the head. On a breezy day plates travel far and it could easily happen. Plastic or Melaware plates don't throw so easily so please don't use them either.

There is a wonderful alternative: the thickish, strong 'paper' plates now sold for picnic and holiday use, and indeed all outdoor needs at any time. They last a long time and don't damage easily, and you can throw them beautifully over long distances, curling away in the sun and the breeze. Buy a packet and put them in the games bag for holiday use on any wide, open space such as a field. Don't throw them in parks though; even a paper plate can hit someone in the eye, or they might scare little children or elderly people out for a walk.

To make a game of it, let everybody throw from the same place and let the winner be the one whose plate travels the farthest distance at one drop. What matters is the first point of contact with the ground, not where the plate finally ends up after rolling.

If the day is fine, bright and sunny there are few games which give you more fun than Aeroplates. To be certain whose plate is whose, write your name boldly on the back with a felt marking pencil.

Measure out distances thrown in paces for quickness.

If you want a very good discus for use in wide, open spaces there is a soft plastic one sold in good sports shops

and toy shops called the 'Frisby' or the 'Getaway'. Its
special aerodynamic shape and design will make it skim
beautifully when thrown with discretion. It returns to the
thrower like a boomerang and almost seems to hover in the
air. It can be used in many outdoor games at camp or on
picnics, and could be a sensation on a wide, broad beach so
long as there are not too many people about.

Elements

This is said to be a quiet game but it can get as fast and
furious as any other. The players form a semi-circle, sitting
on the ground. The leader can stand a short distance away
facing them with a bean bag or a football case stuffed with
an old towel or two. Alternatively, he can stand in the centre
of a larger circle of players. It just depends on how many
you have available.

The leader throws the bag or case-ball to any one player
shouting 'Earth!' as he does so. The player must immediately shout back the name of an animal which lives in the
earth, which for all practical purposes can be any animal
which lives in the wild state above, on, or below the ground.
But it must be an animal. If the leader shouts 'Air!' it has to
be a bird, and if he shouts 'Water!' then it must be a fish or
any animal or mammal which lives in the sea, such as a
whale or a seal, or one which lives in a river, such as an
otter.

If the leader shouts 'Fire!' the person concerned must
whistle loudly for a fire-engine, but he can, if he wishes,
adopt a more modern method and imitate the wailing noise
of an approaching fire-engine at speed.

Play the game first to get used to it and then make a strict
rule that no animal, bird or fish must be mentioned more
than once. This is harder to play than you think.

Rings and Lobs

You can make up a game with practically nothing at all in

S—C

the garden or on a picnic. Simply mark out a rough circle about the size of a dustbin lid with your heel or a sharp stick or a pencil. Then stand at varying distances from it and see how many times you can lob a stone or a plimsoll into it. That's better than nothing but we can improve on it.

It is more fun to lob a stone in a sling underarm than to throw it direct. You can make a sling very easily from an ancient handkerchief or a few pieces of discarded kitchen curtains or *anything*!

Simply tie your stone in one corner so that you can use the rest of the square to lob the stone underarm into the

circle. On a hot day it is more fun to lob stones-in-a-sling into a plastic bucket of water on the lawn or the beach. Anyone who misses three times running can then have the bucket emptied over them as a forfeit – if you are dressed for water fun! – and must go and get it filled up again!

Now try something more difficult. If you have a light-weight plastic lid on your dustbin at home, you can easily work out a circle by putting it down in a suitable place and sticking a few old plastic coloured knitting needles in the

ground at the edge here and there. Then take the lid up and
put it back on the dustbin. Then press these old coloured
knitting needles more firmly in the ground and add as many
more as you can manage within the circle. Also as many old
metal meat skewers as you can find (a few metal tent-pegs
will do instead).

You should soon have a spiky circle bristling with
coloured plastic knitting needles, meat skewers, and so on.
Now you have to stand a fair distance back – mark it with a
rope on the lawn or grass, or a line on the sand – and throw
rubber hoop-la rings over a needle, skewer or tent-peg. Your
score after, say, five throws one after the other can be
counted up according to the colour of the needles. Red is the
most common colour so that's only worth one point. Green
might be two, yellow three, blue four, and so on. The scarcer
the colour the higher the points for ringing it.

The skewers can all be three each as they will be at an
angle and not so easy to ring. Tent-pegs perhaps one each if
they are fairly stout ones.

Keep a proper score card and let everybody have a real go
in turn – perhaps twenty throws in all in four sets of five so
that there is a change of thrower every five shots.

The winner can have anything delicious that is made like
a ring – a gooey doughnut or a frankfurter sausage pinned
up with a toothpick. And we must have a forfeit! A boy can
have a couple of elastic bands put on his ears for a couple of
minutes. No need to worry about forfeits for girls with this
game – they always win it!

Don't forget to wipe the knitting needles clean afterwards
and keep them safely for another day. Meat skewers and
metal tent-pegs need just a touch of white vaseline to keep
them in trim and free from rust.

Outdoor Kim
Kim's Game is a simple way of training you to notice things
speedily. You collect a number of articles, look at them for

two or three minutes, cover them up and then remember what they were and their position. Outdoors on a family picnic you can have a lot of fun with Kim by taking a simple draught board with you, the kind that folds in two with well-marked large squares for draughts.

Collect small items around your picnic site and put them on the draught board in the squares. Pebbles, especially if coloured, shells, small pieces of stone or quartz are ideal. Add coins from Dad's pocket, the tops off soft-drinks bottles, corks – always lots of them about. A paper-clip, pencil-sharpener, eyebath from the first-aid kit, rubber – in fact, anything small that anyone in the family might have about them.

When the draught board is full, put it on the ground and look at it hard for three minutes, memorizing all the items and the positions they were in, eg, third row from the top, third from the right – a small aluminium pencil-sharpener!

The leader covers the board up with a headscarf or large handkerchief and you have to write down all the items on the board in five minutes or less. Prize for the most accurate list, of course. A Coca-Cola will do!

Wild Flower Kim

This is played exactly as Outdoor Kim except that all the items on the draught board squares are small wild flowers. Don't worry if you can't identify all the flowers – perhaps you can look them up another day in any wild flower reference book. It is important not to pick rare wild flowers but it is unlikely that you would be picnicking in a place where rare flowers would be growing.

It is best to collect flowers of differing colours – blue, pink, white, yellow. Later you can, perhaps, press them between sheets of clean white blotting paper and keep them in a little album. You can buy delightful small photo albums now at the gift counters at large stores and multiple chemists very cheaply. They are made in Norway and will take your pressed flowers in the plastic envelope-style pages with a stiff white postcard or plain white card in each envelope-page. This enables you to have two pressed flowers in each well-protected page – you can write on the card the name of the flower and the date of your picnic. This will make Wild Flower Kim an outdoor game to remember!

Tree Kim
This fine outdoor game is played exactly as Wild Flower Kim on a draught board placed on the ground or a checkboard pattern roughly drawn out with a dibber. Simply collect twenty-four leaves of trees, or as many as you can find. Identify them with the help of a reference book and memorize their shapes and special features. Tree Kim will help you. In the spring and autumn you can add the flowers of some trees, and the seeds or fruit, to the leaves. That makes the game even more interesting.

Wild Grass Kim
I always let part of my garden grow quite wild so that the birds can feast on natural seeds and food. Often the wild grasses are among the most beautiful plants in the garden. You can collect and press grasses just the same as flowers. There are so many varieties of grass that you can easily play Outdoor Kim using grasses only.

Fly Casting
This contest can be played by either keen anglers with proper rods and lines or by non-anglers with equipment made simply from garden canes and string. Basically, it is to try and hit a target with the weighted end of a fishing line. If proper rods and lines are to be used, then a target should be laid on the ground between 15 and 20 yards away; for the cane and string contest, 6 or 7 yards distance will be ample. The target can be an old tyre, a hoop, or even a sheet of

newspaper pegged down. Better still, if any water is available the target should be floated on it. The depth of the water should be found and then the target anchored in a suitable spot by two strings with a brick on the end of each. The game can be improved by using five targets at varying distances and giving five points for the farthest, four for the next, and so on. Each competitor has five casts.

'Murps'

Whatever happened to Marbles? It was a great game when I was a boy in Lancashire and North Wales and we spent many happy hours playing endless varieties of 'Murps' – the universal name for it then – on summer evenings on the village greens, and in the parks, and on beaches.

The most popular game then was 'Parky No Sticky' but I could not begin to tell you the complicated rules of how we played it! I am happy to see marbles of all sorts back in the games shops – red and green ones exactly as yesteryear and the lovely coloured glass ones.

If you play marbles, keep them in a wash-leather or thick cotton bag with a drawcord top. Put your initials on the bag – chalk will do.

The best games are the simple ones. A hole with a rounded lip in some firm ground, and a well-marked line 6 feet or so away on which you kneel or stand to make your 'throw'. Start with two, three and four marbles each. Red for you, green for your opponent. As in golf, it is the least number of strokes that matter so if your 'murps' don't all go into the hole at one throw, and they won't, you flick them in with a few well-directed nudges of forefinger and thumb, making a note of the number necessary to achieve the full throw. The position of the thumb and forefinger for flicking is shown in the diagram.

Marbles can get quite exciting when you are throwing with, say, six to ten marbles at a time. The skill lies in nudging your marbles into the hole without putting your opponents' marbles in too. 'In-off' is allowed by the way.

Now clear the decks, and blow your warning whistles! It is my throw ... marvellous, three first time. What did I tell you? Experience counts! But you can beat that easily with a bit of practice.

Write a Line

Occasionally, a writing game is a very good idea – on, say, a wet day near the end of a very active holiday. In this game everybody takes part and writes down two or three sentences of dialogue on separate bits of paper. Anything such as 'Which one sells baked beans, please?', or 'And how far is it to the station?', or 'We have now arrived at the nearest point to the Tower of London'. The leader collects them all up and has to make a running story, reading aloud, from all the slips of paper in his or her possession. He can read any slip twice or more often if he wishes. It is always a very funny game.

Here is a typical recent holiday one:

'How now, brown cow?'

'Feeling beautiful now the rain's stopped!'

'It's been so hot. I can do with a shower.'

'Is it time for dinner yet?'

'Not today, Eustace, surely?'

'What happened to all those baked beans?'

'Dad mixed them with the petrol by mistake.'

'When are we going to the jungle?'

'Any minute now, I should think.'

'I want my dinner!'

'It's a pity Mary isn't here.'

'What's that curious thing behind the hedge?'

'A pork pie – it was in the fridge six months.'

'Go and get yourself de-frosted.'

'I couldn't care less, you know.'

'Can I have my nail-file back?'

'Impossible. I gave it to the vicar for the jumble sale last week.'

'I want my dinner!'

'Who is going to say grace? Will you, Penelope?'

'I say, *Never* let your braces dangle.'

And so on . . .

Pandemonium

This takes a little organizing beforehand and it is well to know who will be playing it; the instructions for small children will vary considerably from those given to older children. A slip of paper is given to each player bearing instructions, such as: 'When the whistle blows sit down in the middle of the lawn' or 'Sit on the lowest branch of the apple tree' or 'Stand on your head'. Half the players will receive these instructions while the other half will receive slips saying: 'Don't let anyone sit in the middle of the lawn', 'Prevent anyone sitting in the apple tree', 'Don't let anyone stand on their head'. You can see why it is called Pandemonium! Just keep it short, about one minute is enough. For older children instructions can be given for group projects: 'Find three other players, pick up the rugby ball and score a try on the south edge of the park' with the opposing instructions 'Don't let anyone pick up the rugby ball and score a try on the south edge of the park!'

Bargain Hunting

This is a nice quiet game for all the family and is ideal on holiday. Each player is given five pence and has to go and buy the best bargain he or she can get for the money. This can be either the largest object for the price, or the most valuable – that is, something worth more than five

pence, or even the most, numerically (see who comes back
with five pence worth of Hundreds and Thousands!). The
categories can be decided beforehand and then a time limit
is set. A great deal of fun can be had searching the smaller
shops for bargains, and if there happens to be a jumble sale
on in the vicinity there is sure to be plenty of choice.

CONKERS GALORE!

September and October are the great conker months for
boys and girls lucky enough to live anywhere near horsechestnut trees. Yet I, for one, being a Northerner, was in my
twenties before I even knew what a conker was: we just
didn't have trees in Lancashire that shed such beautiful
dark-brown shiny fat seeds the size of walnuts every year.

Yet what a lot you can do with conkers apart from collecting them, and gloating over their lovely brown shiny skins.
'If only you could eat them!' sighed one girl. But of course
you *can't*! NOT EVER!

Boys can use them as freight in their model-railway
layouts. They are clean and easy to store. And everybody
knows the conker game in which you thread conkers on a
tough piece of parcel string, or cord, and then have a whale
of a time trying to split your friend's conker in two with
well-aimed throws, whirling the conker round your head.
The best knot to secure the conker is the simple overhand
knot pulled extremely tight.

A figure-of-eight knot

The figure-of-eight knot is the best one to stop a conker coming off the end of a length of string, but you will need to pierce the conker very carefully and gently with a thin meat skewer first. Don't be disappointed if you split three or four first.

It's great fun but don't believe any of those stories about pickling your conker in vinegar to get it in even better shape for the great fights. Vinegar does nothing to your conker except spoil and corrode the surface. Better to let the conkers dry off naturally. If it's been a good season they will be large and extra-shiny and stay like that for years. But if there has been a drought in the early and mid-part of the spring and summer, or too much rain in the summer and not enough sun, they will be small and very poor specimens. Never keep small conkers. They are best put somewhere in the garden or park where squirrels will eat them later on.

There are *many* more conker games. For instance, stand in a small circle with your eyes closed and your hands behind your back, each boy or girl holding a conker in each hand. Then pass conkers from hand to hand as rapidly as you can while someone counts aloud and quite quickly up to twenty. The same person feeds extra conkers into the waiting palms of anyone in need! This causes some confusion!

At twenty the game stops and anyone without two conkers, one in each hand, is out. Some mysteriously have more conkers than they started with.

Blind Pirates
This is a conker game for a dry day, since you have to crawl on the ground. Put all the conkers you collect into several small heaps, one pile, say, in the centre of the area where you are going to play – two or three other heaps around but some little distance apart.

Now everybody becomes a Blind Pirate out to collect treasure! (You must be blindfold for this game – hankies, or scarves will do.) The pirates are allowed one last look at the conkers before blindfolding. Turn round on all fours three or four or more times and then on the word 'Go!' and only on all fours, you must try and find the conker heaps and make a collection of, say, ten conkers.

The conkers must be stuffed in pockets, or a sock gripped in your teeth (*yes!*) or *anything*. The first one to shout 'Ten' is the winner.

Conker Century

The conkers must be placed in four heaps at the four corners (bases) of a fairly large square – say, 30 yards each side. Now each boy and girl sets off running in turn from first base to second base picking up five conkers *at each one*, then on to the third and fourth base. He or she should now have twenty conkers which is quite a lot to handle at a time (unless you have *very* big hands). If the player has less than twenty he can only chart up the number held in two hands at the finale – say, fourteen or fifteen.

In all, each boy or girl has five runs round the square and the eventual winner is the one who has the nearest figure to one hundred – which is the maximum you can get, of course. Anything over sixty is good.

You can make this game as difficult as you like, or easier for younger children. It is a very good game for autumn picnics.

Conker Batman

This game, appealing mostly to boys, is the same game as a popular beach game with a tennis ball and cricket bat when there are only two players. But it can be played by any reasonably small number, say, three, four or five players.

The conkers used must be hard and firm or else they will split and be useless – which means they must be dry. A boy, armed with a boy's size cricket bat, throws a conker up in the air and has to hit it as far as he can in a stated direction. It isn't that easy to hit a conker, in fact. A tennis ball is much easier. The winner is the boy who after an agreed number of hits – say, four, five or six – hits a conker the farthest distance in paces. A game for plenty of space and best supervised by Dad, just to stop any arguments. May the best Batsman win!

Conker Patterns

Girls love to make patterns with conkers. Sometimes you collect hundreds and hundreds. Make patterns with them on the ground such as cartwheels, clock faces, chess-board squares, diamond-mesh patterns, compasses, playing-card patterns, and so on. This is a good game when you collect lots of conkers of different sizes.

Hot Potato

More suitable for younger children than Hot Rice (page 75). Everybody sits down in a circle facing inwards. One boy or girl stands up in the centre. A conker (or you can use a bean bag, or old football-case stuffed with a towel) is thrown or passed from one player to another across or round the circle out of reach of the player in the centre. He or she tries to intercept. If successful, then he or she takes the place of the thrower and so it goes on. The object passed round or tossed about must not be a ball which will bounce.

Grab!

A simple game popular with young boys. Some older person sits on a stool, rock or fence, or anything available, with a large bag of conkers on his lap. Any number of players sit around in a halfmoon circle about 5 yards away. The Conker King now tells, or reads, some simple adventure story using the word 'Grab!' as much as possible – putting it in the text and dialogue wherever possible. This can be very funny. Wherever he says 'Grab!' he throws one or more conkers in the circle which are seized by the first boy who can get to it – standing up not allowed, of course. At the end of the story the winner is the boy with the greatest number of conkers.

No Litter, Please

As you know conkers are seeds. They fall naturally to the ground when they are ready – so don't try to speed up Nature's wonderful process by trying to knock down conkers before they are ready to fall – the result is always poor-quality conkers. The conkers are encased in a bright-green outer skin known usually as a 'conker shell'.

Don't ever leave these skins or shells lying around after you have collected your conkers. They make a ghastly mess if you do and can be quite dangerous to elderly people in wet weather if they tread on them on a walk through the park or around the common. Collect all the skins or shells you can and put them in the litter baskets provided or in a neat pile where the groundsmen will find them.

At home you can put all your shells on the compost heap or bonfire. Don't leave them lying around the garden. As for the conkers you collect, in time you get tired of them. If you have collected them and not dried them properly they will go mouldy. Put them in the kitchen boiler and hear them pop. If you have central heating and no fireplaces or boilers, the dustbin is the only answer.

Finally, there are plenty of places in Britain where children never see conkers, especially in dockland towns, fishing ports and big cities. Send them some as a gift with toys and books at Christmas. Your church will help you to find a home. I once lived for six weeks in a settlement for homeless boys in a drab part of London's East End. They enjoyed the bags of conkers I took them most of all!

On the day I wrote this I was fascinated to watch a young grey squirrel eating conkers in my garden. He would climb high up into a horsechestnut tree, and preen himself like a cat, washing behind both ears and also grooming his tail. Then he would select a conker in its green skin or shell and detach it carefully from the tree, finally carrying it down to a lower branch where he carefully peeled it, first the green shell and then the whole of the brown shiny skin. Then he raced madly into another tree and ate every bit of the pale-green peeled conker. In my part of the world, grey squirrels are not a pest and the few we have are always interesting to watch. I hope there will always be enough conkers left on the trees to provide a bit of lunch when required.

Acorns

Acorns can be found almost everywhere and no boy or girl can resist collecting them. Many of the games I have suggested for conkers can all be played with acorns equally well and they make wonderful ballast for any model-railway layout. I like to put small heaps of them under leaves and garden clippings for the winter. Then, when all food is scarce for wild creatures, I give them a few handfuls at a time which all helps them to survive another winter.

Apple Bobbing

When there are plenty of apples about – especially, in the autumn – Apple Bobbing is a good game for the garden, and possibly the park if the attendants will allow you to tie an apple on to a suitable tree branch. Always ask first.

The apple selected should be a crisp, sweet one (modesty will not allow me to mention a famous pippin of world renown) and it should not be too big either.

Tie the apple firmly to a length of thin cord with an over-hand knot and then tie the cord with a round turn and two half-hitches (see diagram) to a tree branch or suitable alternative. The same figure-of-eight knot used in the conker games will stop your apple falling off the cord if you prefer to put a hole through it with a skewer.

Players take it in turn to try and eat the apple with hands

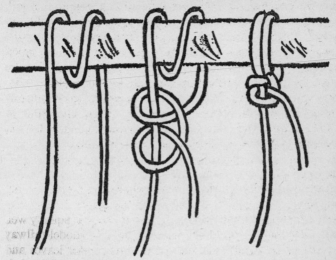

tied behind their back. You will have to adjust the cord length according to the height of the children taking part.

Finally in our section on games for parks and gardens, what about holding a . . .

MINI-OLYMPICS!

A scaled-down version of athletics, suitable for the garden or park. Events have the same names as their big brothers, but are really just for fun. Here are a few well-tried and popular contests, others can be invented quite easily. The idea is that the best athlete, or the biggest or oldest competitor, is not necessarily going to be the winner, which can be boring for everyone.

Javelin

Each competitor is given a piece of paper 12 inches square and they have to make it up into a paper dart or plane. The object is to either see who can throw their javelin the farthest from a starting line, or see who can complete a course with the lowest number of throws. Naturally, the 'javelins' will fly all over the place, which just adds to the fun. If a course is used it can be straight, crooked, circular or square. All competitors throw together and then go to where their javelin lands for the next throw. Competitors throw together at all times and in this way a check can be kept on the number of throws taken.

Discus
Use paper plates, ice-cream tub tops, or anything similar and play it just like the javelin contest. Be careful when throwing not to hit anyone.

Putting the Shot
Obviously a weight cannot be used for this mini-Olympic game so the answer is to use a feather! Play just like javelin.

Long Jump
Choose a suitable piece of ground, preferably with some soft sand that will show up where competitors land, near a wall, fence, tree, or even where there is a large stone or piece of wood. Competitors stand with their heels pressed firmly against the object and then make a feet-together jump forwards as far as they can go. Knees are not allowed to be bent at all, which is why the game is best played from a wall. The idea is to let the body fall forward until it is on the point of overbalancing then leap forward with both feet. Mark where the heels of each competitor land to decide the winner.

High Jump
This is slightly more difficult to stage and needs a system of handicapping if there is any great variation in the height of the contestants. A circle about 12 inches in diameter is marked out on the ground and a string is stretched over

about 18 inches above the heads of the contestants. The idea is to make a feet-together standing jump upwards and try to touch the string with the head. The handicapping system will have to be worked out so that smaller players can either stand on something to bring them up to the height of the taller players, or the string must be lowered an equal number of inches. Raise the string each time a player touches it until a winner is found.

Four-legged Race
There are obviously all sorts of variations on a straight running race – hopping, running backwards, and so on – but one, which really has no equivalent in the real Olympic Games, is great fun for spectators and players. It is a *Four-legged Race*. Three competitors form a team and the legs of the centre man are tied firmly to the left and right legs of the two outside runners, just like a three-legged race – but much funnier! You can, of course, make a five-, six-, or even more-legged race.

Show Jumping
Competitors are teamed up as horses and riders and have to complete a course of 'fences' – sticks across two large stones or bricks, and so on – and points are deducted for every obstacle knocked down. The poor horse is not expected to jump the obstacles, which should only be about 1 foot high, but the fences should be so arranged that careful stepping is required to get over them. Two fences can be set so close together that the horses' feet will have to be turned sideways to get between them, or there can be a 'water jump' marked out on the ground that takes a really long stride to cross. One fence should be set about 4 feet high so that the horse and rider have to duck under without dislodging the pole – a garden bamboo cane is best here – and without the rider or any part of the horse except his feet touching the ground. Other obstacles will suggest themselves, according to where the event is held.

Rowing

Teams of two competitors who sit on the ground facing each other. Each grasps the other's upper arm and moves forwards until they are sitting on each other's feet. The competitor with his back to the course rocks backwards and stands up, straightening his knees as he does so, and then sits down again, still on his partner's feet, which moves him a few inches up the course. As he sits down he pulls his partner up and then, as his partner sits down, closer to him, he starts the rocking motion over again until a rhythm is set up and they go rocking down the course.

Archery

Each competitor will need a strong rubber band and some paper to be folded into pellets. Six corks are stood on a wall and contestants have six shots each at them by hooking the band over their fingers and thumbs and using the paper pellets as catapult missiles.

Foul-play Race

No biting, kicking or scratching – but everything else goes in this race. Mark out a course for an ordinary running race, about 50 yards or twice round the garden is sufficient, and have the contestants lined up at the start. The aim is to win the race by preventing anyone else getting to the winning post first. Players may tackle each other, trip, or drag each other back until one manages to break away and reach home. Stop the game immediately this happens!

Horse Feathers

This game got its name because it is a pillow fight on horseback, and if a pillow bursts . . . It is a game that is fun for players and spectators. Some apparatus is needed and a little preparation but if the game is to be played in the garden, the equipment can be left up and used over and over again. The 'horse' is a thick pole or log at least 6 feet long supported at either end by a trestle so that it is about 4 feet off the ground. Ideally, the centre part should swivel so that contestants will fall off but as this is not practicable for most people the best idea is to wrap the pole with polythene sheeting; any large bags, opened up and tied or taped on firmly will do. The ground beneath the horse should be spread with mats or something soft to act as a breakfall. Two players take part at a time and each is given a pillow or cushion. They climb aboard the horse from opposite ends and edge their way forward until they can swing the pillows at each other and attempt to knock each other off. If any part of a player touches the ground he must retire, or if he swings under the horse and cannot get back to an upright position by a count of ten, during which his opponent must refrain from attacking him, he has lost. The winner remains on the horse and another challenger takes over until a champion is found. A simpler way of suspending the horse is if a convenient tree can be found when the pole or log is hung by a strong rope from either end to a branch above. This is even funnier because the horse bucks and sways each time the horsemen take a swing at each other.

4 GAMES OF STRENGTH

Quarter Staffs
This is one of the oldest games known in Britain and still gives lots of fun. All you need is a pair of stout sticks about 4 feet long. Two boys or girls face each other holding the sticks firmly with both hands near each end. Then they cross the sticks at right angles to start the game and begin.

You have to force your opponent over with various ploys, always making sure that at all times you both grasp the sticks with both hands. It is surprising how long you go on before one of the players has to admit defeat.

Then you start again or someone else takes over. A really warming game for winter, or for a cool spring or autumn day when you have gone in search of a good picnic spot.

Sprint Tug O'War

A line is drawn across the games area and a length of rope for tug o' war is laid along it. A handkerchief or something similar is tied round the rope to mark the centre. Two teams line up at opposite ends of the area and, on the starting signal, they run forward, grab the rope and attempt to get it back to their own end. Be sure that each team knows which end of the rope is theirs; they must not touch the rope on the other side of the handkerchief. The winning team is the one that touches *any part* of the rope down on the ground at their own end, so some form of boundary line should be marked at each end.

Over My Shoulder

Two boys stand back to back, feet well braced. They should be roughly the same size in height and weight. They put their arms out wide and grasp each other's fingers. On the word 'Go!' they shove each other like mad each trying to force the other over his shoulder. It's marvellous exercise and best played in a sandy spot or anywhere where soft landings can be guaranteed.

Just the job before a swim, to limber you up!

Trust (also known as Trust your Weight)

This game has long been popular in the North but is more suitable for, say, a family camping holiday in which (with guests) there may be several boys around the same age. A game, I would say, for the ten to fifteen age range. The minimum number required is four, and it is excellent for six boys. Split into two equal-in-size units of two or three boys or what is available. Then toss a coin for first 'go'.

The losing side, if you can call two or three boys a side, make a 'wall' end-on against a tree or fence of some kind or a haystack. One boy stands head down against the tree, fence or stack, with his elbows up and hands clasped over his neck. His companions stand behind him holding firmly on to his waist. The 'wall' is rather like a buck, pommel or 'horse' in the gym to look at. All heads are well down.

The first time down is a low 'wall' and progressively the 'walls' are higher, as high as the boys can make it, in fact.

Now the first boy from the side which won the toss has to run, perhaps 10 yards, and jump on to the wall and hang on, or make a glorious leapfrog jump which takes him on to the shoulders of the first boy in the wall. The second boy makes his run and jump, and the third if you are lucky enough to have three in each side.

The 'wall' has to hold while someone counts or checks a watch. It is a case of Trust, that is Trust your Weight, hence the name. After four or five progressively more difficult jumps as the 'wall' gets higher, the other side has a go and wins if it stays, in all, longer off the ground.

Top Dog

Another game of strength chiefly for boys. Two of the same age and size and weight can play at a time. Find a place where you can fall without hurting yourself – such as a sandy dune, or a grassy hill slope.

You stand side by side with your legs slightly apart and well braced. Then one of you tries to get the leg which is alongside your companion's leg quickly locked with his leg so that he is thrown – gently – backwards. This can be quite a trial of strength and makes you quite breathless. But it is very good for growing leg muscles and sinews!

When you have had enough you should each have been

Top Dog about an equal number of times. If this isn't the case, then one of you is too strong for the other and you can't be very equal yet. No matter. You will be soon.

Chinese Boxing

Chinese Boxing has long been a boys' favourite. You get a lot of fun and exercise without hurting each other at all and you certainly don't have to wear any boxing-gloves. Two boys face each other and grasp each other's right (left) wrist with the left (right) hand very firmly. They should be about a yard apart, no more.

The right (left) arms are held firmly straight out at the level of the shoulder. Now the game can begin. On the word 'Go!' each boy tries to 'hit' (smack would be a better word) the other with the right (left) hand, at the same time pushing the other's right (left) hand away.

It is strenuous fun and it may be that you are better at it one side rather than the other. That is why I have put the opposite word in brackets in the description so that you can try it both ways.

To get the real atmosphere you need to wear some baggy silk pantaloons with a few clanging cymbals but for a picnic in the park, or a sunny morning on the beach, I think we'll stick to what we've got, don't you?

Chinese Wrestling

Two players stand back to back, bend down and grasp each other's hands through their legs and try to pull each other over a marked line.

Wristo!

Two players lie flat on their stomachs, facing each other, and place their right elbows on the ground and grasp hands. The object is to force the opponent's hand down until the back of it touches the ground. The elbows must be kept on the ground at all times.

Buster
Players stand chest to chest with arms outstretched to the sides and grasp hands. They rest their chins on their opponent's shoulder and then attempt to push him backwards to a marked line, keeping the arms out at the side and using the chest only for pushing.

Indian Leg Wrestling
Two players lie down side by side but with their heads at opposite ends. The right legs are raised and each hooks the other one behind the knee. The object is by using the leg only to turn the opponent on his side.

Heave-Ho!
Players sit on the ground opposite each other with the soles of their feet pressed together. They grasp hands and each attempts to make the other lift his bottom off the ground by pulling.

Ankle Tapping
This was a favourite game with Scouts in the days when staves were carried. It needs speed and a quick eye. Two sticks about an inch or so in diameter and 5 feet long are needed; heavy enough so that two hands must be employed to use them. Each player takes a stick, taps the ground three times in front of him to show he is ready and then tries to tap his opponent's ankles. The first player to score three taps is the winner. The stick may be jabbed or swept round but it must not go above knee height and two hands must be used all the time.

Hoop Wrestling
Two players stand in a hoop, tyre or circle drawn on the ground and wrestle to try and make their opponent put a foot outside. Arms and bodies only are allowed to be used, no feet. Best of three games is the winner.

Ankle Grab

Two players kneel and face each other, preferably in a circle of other players, and try to grab each other's ankle. They must not rise from their knees but can lay on the ground. As soon as an ankle is grasped, not just touched, the winner challenges another player in the circle until a champion is found.

Tail Tag

This can be played by two or more players, or in the manner of Ankle Grab. Players have a handkerchief, scarf or piece of string tucked loosely in the back of their belt or tucked into the waistband of their skirt or shorts, jeans or trousers. Their opponent tries to steal the 'tail', while defending his own. Winner can be the player who collects the most tails, or it can be played as a partners' game until a champion is decided.

Triangle Tug O' War

A game for three players. A long piece of rope and three objects are needed — spades, buckets, stones, hats, or anything similar. The rope's ends are joined together to make a loop and the three players grasp it in one hand at equal distances from each other. One of the objects is placed behind each player but about a yard out of reach. The game is for each player to pull against the others and try to pick up his object.

Push O' War

Teams are selected of equal size and weight, just as in a normal tug o' war, and the players of each team stand side by side, facing the other team. Players should be lined up so that their opponents are of the same height and weight, as near as possible. A rope is laid on the ground between the two teams and on the command they pick up the rope and try to push it to a marked area about 10 feet behind the opposing team. Any part of the rope that touches the area counts as a win.

HORSE AND RIDER GAMES

These are great favourites and capable of many variations. One thing that must be decided first is whether the horse and the rider are going to change places at any time. If so, the two players must be of equal weight. The other thing to be decided in all 'fighting' games is whether or not the horses are allowed to fight.

Pull Down

This is simply a free-for-all in which all horses and riders attempt to pull each other down. When a rider touches the ground, he and his horse drop out.

Couples

This is the team version of Pull Down, useful for a get-together with large numbers. Two teams of horses and riders line up facing each other with the heaviest pairs at *opposite* ends of their teams and the line graduated down to the lightest player. The heavy pairs in each team are number one, and so on down the line. The leader calls a number and the two opposing sets of players with that number move into the centre of the lines and attempt to pull each other down. The leader may call more than one number but only players with the same number will attack each other.

Horse Tally-ho

A horse and rider are placed in the centre of the games area and all the other horses and riders line up at one end. These are numbered from one onwards. The leader, or the rider in the centre, calls a number and the horse and rider with that number attempt to run through to the other end. If they are pulled down by the centre pair, they also go into the centre and help catch other players. If the pair get through to the other end the rider calls 'Tally-ho!' and all the horses and riders at the far end gallop through while the centre pairs try to pull them down. Then the game goes on until the last pair are caught.

Run and Mount

A line is drawn across the centre of the games area (on grass use the plastic white clothes-line). All the horses and riders then form two circles at one end, riders in the centre, horses on the outside. At the leader's signal they start to walk round, horses clockwise, riders anti-clockwise. The leader will call 'Run', and the players run, and then 'Mount'. Each rider must find his horse, mount him and race to the far end of the area. The last pair across the centre line drops out.

Rats and Rabbits

Best played in two small teams. Two teams of horses and riders face each other about 4 feet apart. The riders are dismounted and standing behind their horses. One team is Rats and the other Rabbits. The leader calls out either 'Rats' or 'Rabbits' and the team named must run away to the end of the area behind them while the opposing team chases them. No player may move unless mounted. Any pair touched by a chaser is captured and joins the opposing team. Any pair who runs the wrong way – runs *forwards* when his team is called, or *away* when the opposing team is called – is counted as captured and immediately joins the opposing team. A canny leader will build up the tensions by stringing out the names – 'rrrrrrrrrrrrrats!' or even an occasional 'rrrrrrrrrraspberry!'

Rat Race

This is a variation on Rats and Rabbits. Two lines are marked across the centre of the area about 4 feet apart and a second line marked 18 inches behind each of them. The two teams line up behind the second lines, dismounted, and a bean bag, hank of rope, rubber quoit or something similar is placed at the feet of the horse in one team. The player attempts to kick the object into the 'tramlines' in front of the opposing team and if *any* part of the object stays within the tramlines, the kicking team mount up and run away and the other team chase them. The same rules apply as in Rats and Rabbits. If the object does not land in the tramline it is passed to the first horse in the opposing team for a kick, and then backwards and forwards to alternate teams.

5 CIRCLE GAMES

Twos and Threes
A game for an even number of players. All choose partners
and form a circle facing inwards, one player standing behind
his partner. Two of the players become hunter and hunted
and run round the circle and in and out of the players. If the

hunted is touched, the roles are reversed and the hunted
becomes the hunter. At any time the hunted may stand in
front of any couple, making three, and the rear player then
becomes the hunted and runs away, until he, too, is either
touched by the hunter or stands in front of another couple.
Make sure that the same pair do not continue to play for too
long.

Slap the Slipper

Players form a circle and stand with their eyes closed and their hands behind their backs. One player walks quietly round the outside of the circle carrying a slipper and places it in the hands of one of the players. As soon as he does he must continue in the same direction round the circle with the other player chasing him and trying to slap him with the slipper. He attempts to get back into the place vacated by the chaser but if he is slapped he once again takes over the slipper. If he gets home safely the chaser walks round with the slipper for the next turn.

Chase the Thimble

For this party game you really need something a little larger than a thimble – a plastic tumbler, for instance, but almost anything fairly soft and unbreakable will do. The players are divided into two, three, or even more, equal teams and each member is given a number. Keeping in numerical order, the teams sit in one large circle and the 'thimble' is placed in the centre. The umpire calls a number and the players from each team who have that number leap to their feet and run in a clockwise direction round the circle, back to their own place and try to grab the thimble. First player to do so gains a point for his team. This is a very good game for an outing with another family.

Human Chair

This is not so much a game as an odd-minute gag. All the players form a circle standing one behind the other. Then everyone sits down on the knees of the player behind . . . until the whole circle forms a human chair. There are no winners – just see how long the chair can be kept up.

Tree Ball

Players stand in a large circle round a tree and one player stands in the middle as defender. The circle of players throws a ball to try and hit the tree, not above shoulder height, and the defender tries to stop the ball. If the tree is hit, the thrower claims a point; if the defender touches the ball, the player who threw it becomes defender. The player with the most points after a set time is the winner.

Poison Pool

Here is a game for three or more players that requires quite a bit of agility. The players form a circle round a chair, stool, or even a sheet of newspaper held down by stones. This is the Poison Pool and anyone touching it loses a life. The object is for the players to hold hands and try to pull each other onto it. If any players cross over the Pool without touching it, the game stops and the circle is reformed round the Pool. Players have a number of lives agreed on before the game starts – three is usually sufficient – and they lose one each time they touch the Pool. A life is also lost by *both* players who release their hold on each other, so a good grip is necessary. The best way is to hold each others' wrists.

Jump the Rope

Players stand in a circle round a central player who holds a rope with a soft weight on the end. This can be a bundle of cloth, or a very large knot on the end of the rope itself, or best of all, a rubber quoit. The player in the middle swings the rope round slowly at ankle height and the circle of players have to jump over it as it passes. The rope is gradually speeded up and raised until it is knee height. Any player touched by the rope or weight either loses a life or drops out of the game, whichever is decided beforehand. Each player can have three lives and drops out when they are lost. The player in the centre will get dizzy very quickly so change places frequently, perhaps making the rule that any player hit by the rope takes over in the centre.

Spincatcher

This is a game for a hot afternoon when you don't want to do very much. Just sit round in a rough circle – as many of you as want to play. One person holds an enamel or plastic plate in his hand on its edge so that one edge is touching the sand or the ground – and you need a firm, flat, hard surface. He spins the plate rapidly so that it turns like a top. This is not at all difficult and with a little practice you can become very good at it indeed.

As he starts the spin he calls someone's name and he or she must dive forward and grab the plate before the spin has gone and it falls to the ground! Not that easy really but great fun. If the person named fails, he or she spins the plate and calls someone else's name, and so on.

I don't think you need any prizes or forfeits for this game. It's just a pleasant way of making the best possible use of a plate on a very hot day. It's always the youngest members of the family who seem to win, by the way. No use asking me to play. I've fallen asleep, until teatime. I don't grunt or snore either. Only *snort*.

Bull's Eye

This game is more suited for a farm holiday because you need an old bucket to stand on and you are more likely to find one – if the farmer agrees to let you use it – on a farm than a beach or a park open space. It is a simple game but always good fun, with as many players as you like. First to bat stands on the bucket with any kind of cricket bat in his hand, or an old tennis racket if you like, or any kind of improvised bat.

The rest of the players stand in a circle round the bucket at a reasonable distance, say 3 or 4 yards, less if you like, or more. The ball is our old favourite tennis or sorbo ball. The thrower is only allowed to throw underarm and has to try and hit the bucket.

The batsman has to prevent the bowler or thrower from

doing this. If he stops it with his bat, he counts one run. If the ball misses the bucket entirely, nothing is counted. The batsman is out if the ball hits the bucket or if he is caught. And there can be quick inter-passing of the ball among the bowlers in the circle to keep the batsman on the alert. It's an old favourite, excellent for a wet day played in a Dutch barn under cover. Forfeit for a duck! Stand on the bucket on one leg for a whole minute.

Another version of this game is popular in the South of England:

Bucket Cricket

This is played exactly as Hot Rice (2) (see page 76) except that the defender stands on an upturned bucket. If he is hit on the legs with the ball, or if he steps off the bucket, he must immediately drop the bat and the first player to get it becomes defender.

Smash and Grab

This is a sort of mini-rounders. A short, thick stick and a soft ball are required. The players stand in a circle and one takes the bat. Any player can toss the ball into the air in the circle and the batsman strikes at it. If he misses three times, he drops the bat and the first player to pick it up becomes the batsman.

If he hits the ball, the other players attempt to catch it and the player who does so becomes the batsman. If nobody catches it, the first player to reach the ball holds it up. The players move away to give him a clear shot and the batsman lays the bat on the ground. The player with the ball then throws it at the bat and, if he hits it, he becomes batsman. If he misses, the same batsman continues with three more strikes at the ball. Any player may serve but fair tosses must be given.

Hot Rice (1)

A *soft* ball and some form of bat are needed. A circle about

12 inches diameter is drawn on the ground and one player holds the bat and stands in the circle; the remaining players form a large circle around him and care should be taken that this circle does not get smaller. The aim is for the circle of players to throw the ball at the legs of the man in the middle and he to defend his legs with the bat. He may turn whichever way he likes *but he must keep one foot in the small circle.* The player who succeeds in hitting the defender's legs takes his place.

Hot Rice (2)

This is a faster version of Hot Rice and is played mainly in the North of England. The batsman can move *anywhere* within a large circle, which must be marked out on the ground and within which all play takes place.

He stands in the middle of the large circle with a boy's size cricket bat and the rest stand round him on the perimeter with a tennis ball. The batsman is out as soon as the ball hits his legs below the knee, and he has to be pretty smart on his feet to survive for long. The ball is likely to come from any angle, so he must watch it like a hawk. If he starts watching the thrower he is lost. He defends his legs with the bat and tries, of course, to hit the ball out of the circle to prolong his life. (Players cannot throw the ball from within the circle.) Hot Rice is best played with a leader who will time the batsman or batsgirl. If he has a stopwatch, wonderful!

Dog in Manger

An old outdoor favourite that has stood the test of time. One boy or girl (the Dog) has to protect a small heap of pebbles, shells, stones, conkers, acorns, building bricks, marbles, or anything similar. A roomy circle is quickly made round the Dog and his or her 'treasure', either with a dibber on sand or a rope or line of stones on grass.

The rest of the players stand outside the circle and have to try to steal some treasure without being touched. They can feint the move they are going to make – run round the circle and dart in – or make a series of lightning pounces. If the Dog touches anyone inside the circle they are out. The Dog wins if all players are out and he or she still has some treasure left.

Mersey Tunnel

All the players available sit down in a circle and breathe in very deeply – you can have a few trial breaths to get used to the idea. As the leader points to someone, he or she has to let out a long whistle as we enter the Mersey Tunnel (make believe, of course) and keep it up as long as possible. That gives you the idea.

Now for the game proper. Everybody breathes in and when the leader raises his arm (he can do this dramatically to add to the fun in a magnificent sweeping gesture) everybody lets out a Mersey Tunnel whistle. Last whistler left wins the coveted chocolate bar, and I am sure he well deserves it.

To leave no one in any doubt about the end of a whistle, a player should collapse flat on his or her back as soon as he or she can whistle no more.

Kim's Compass

This is one of the most successful outdoor games which came to me in a flash of inspiration at a camp years ago. You can play it on any beach with a hard flat sandy surface or a stretch of level not-too-long grass. Let's try it as a beach game first.

Draw a fairly big circle, say, 6 feet in diameter, with the dibber and mark the sixteen points of the compass on it at the correct points in bold capital letters. To get yourself used to the compass, put the North point in the correct place first. Even if it isn't in the *exact* place it doesn't matter for the game.

Next to each compass point put any article you like collected from the family – anything from pockets, handbags, shopping bags or the car. Now memorize the articles and the compass point they are at – such as 'North-east, a lady's blue hankie' – 'South-south-west, green comb', and so on. Look at them hard for three minutes.

Now cover all the items (with towels, groundsheets, newspapers – anything suitable to hand). See how many you can remember in five minutes out of sixteen – remember, the exact compass point and the article. Pop them down on a card or in a notebook.

It isn't difficult to remember those sixteen articles and their positions.

Now add a second circle to the compass about a foot

nearer to the centre of the circle and put another sixteen articles on those new intersecting points. It will help if the articles are related in some way to the articles on the first circle – you can remember *related* articles better. So you will have, say, a small blue hankie on north-east 1 and a white large hankie on north-east 2. A green comb on south-south-west 1 and a black one on south-south-west 2.

Play it the same way. Soon you will be able to remember the names and the positions on the compass of thirty-two articles quite easily.

When you get better at it you can play it with three circles, forty-eight compass points and forty-eight articles – and it is a game every person in the family can play, young and old.

I think it's best played when you have had a lot of running-about fun and are looking for something quieter to do.

Surprising, too, how you get to know your compass points so quickly!

6 BALL GAMES

Lawn (or Beach) Golf

If you have a medium-sized or large lawn at home you can easily rig up various golf games. Probably three or four holes will be all that you can manage on an average-sized lawn but the modern trend is to cut down garden work by having larger lawns so you may be able to manage five or six holes.

Lawn Golf can easily be adapted into Beach Golf. For the lawn at home you will need twice the number of small plastic plant pots (say 3 inches in diameter) per hole. If you have enough space for, say, four holes on the lawn to give you a putting distance of 7 to 10 yards between each on a zig-zag course, you will need eight plastic pots.

You fill one set of four pots with compost or earth up to the brim and these stay in the lawn in the holes which you cut out very carefully with a sharp knife. This enables mowing to proceed. Probably green is the best colour for the pots if you can get it. When you play Lawn Golf you take these pots out and put the other set of empty ones in their place, replacing them with the filled pots when the game is over.

If pots are very scarce you could do the same thing with ice-cream cartons but plastic plant pots are so much easier and look very much better. You can give the game an almost professional touch by using little pennants or flags which you can make yourself to mark each hole. Or any kind of plastic tag on a little stick will do.

Play the game with old golf balls and a couple of old putters, or walking sticks which make an admirable substitute. Proceed from the first to the fourth hole on any kind of route you like. If your lawn has a few hazards of its own, such as a sloping bank, or an odd ornamental bush or rockery, so much the better. You can soon work out your own record scores and par for the course! It is surprising how attractive this little putting game becomes, and you can play it for most of the year, too.

Beach Golf is played the same way with as few players as two, and as many as you like. All you need in this case is an empty ice-cream carton, one for each hole, placed wherever you like. Try and find a firm stretch of sand near the top of the beach where it will be quite firm. If you find putters hard to obtain, use walking sticks or any kind of small children's cricket bats. Old tennis balls are easier to use for younger children than golf balls. It's fun, but remember to keep a proper score card with all golf-type games.

Catch as Catch Can

This is a tennis-ball game which girls like a lot but anyone can play. For a start you can have two girls standing opposite each other, armed with one tennis ball each. On the word 'Go!' they bounce the ball they are holding to each other so that after one bounce fairly near each other – sometimes they do hit each other – the balls are exchanged almost simultaneously. It takes a little practice.

Now try holding one ball in each hand, bouncing one ball to the other using the same sequence: right-left, right-left. It is best done in unison which you can shout to each other 'Right-left, right-left'. The idea is that you work up a rhythmic exchange of tennis balls so that the balls are constantly changing hands.

It's good for your coordination and for your eyes. But it takes longer to achieve smoothness and perfection than you think.

In time you will be able to achieve a very attractive cross pattern with four girls (and eight tennis balls) in a large cross, bouncing two balls to each other in unison. Three minutes without dropping a ball is marvellous!

Patball

If you find Catch as Catch Can too hard, then try Patball. This is simply serving a tennis ball from one person to another either with the hand or a table-tennis bat over an improvised net which can be just a length of white tape, or one end of the white plastic clothes-line from the games bag, suitably tied perhaps from a tree to an iron railing or something similar. There are no elaborate rules or procedures. You just serve to each other and keep the ball in the air as much as possible. If you let the ball drop on your side of the tape, it's a point for your opponent. There are no penalties if by chance a ball goes under the tape. Just start again with an underarm serve every time.

Circle Ball

There are many varieties of ball games called Circle Ball but one very successful one that I have always liked very much can be played anywhere by any number of players.

First of all, you need a base of some kind. This should be

about 3 feet in diameter, roughly the size of a dustbin lid, our old favourite measure. This could be a well-chalked area on a suitably hard surface; but on a beach it could be a circular or square piece of wood (the end of an orange box) . . . anything you may find on the beach. It could also be a suitable piece of packaging carton well bedded into the firm sand. On grass it could again be a suitable piece of wood or hardboard or plastic. Anything that would have a flat surface and remain rigid. If possible, peg it down.

The players then stand round the base in a circle about 7 to 10 yards in diameter, which you will have to judge for yourselves, according to the area available and the age and capacity of your players. One player then has the ball (tennis or sorbo) and has to bounce it to another player on the other side of the circle, so that the ball bounces on the base and is caught first time. Hence, the need for a very flat base or else the ball will bounce oddly.

With practice this game becomes fast and furious as the players bounce balls to each other as quickly as possible, one taking over from another as the ball comes his or her way. There are no winners, points or anything like that. It's just for fun.

French Cricket

As old as the hills but still a very good game for the garden, the park or any stretch of firm grass or beach.

French Cricket is usually played with a small boy's size bat and a tennis ball with the batsman using the bat with two hands in front of him in the standing position to defend his closed legs below the knee, which are, in effect, the wicket. The bowler, using underarm leg breaks or offspinners to good effect, has to hit the legs of the batsman and he bowls from the point at which the ball is fielded after it has been hit. The batsman must stay in the same spot, but he may jump round to face the bowler. Each time he hits the ball, he counts a run.

French Cricket always seems to be heavily weighted in favour of the batsman especially as a tennis ball is used, which does not take kindly to bowling skills on any kind of 'pitch'.

I suggest you use a rounders bat, or an Indian club (if you can lay your hands on one!) instead of a cricket bat, which will make life much more difficult for the batsman. It also puts concentration, which is the outstanding quality of the great game of cricket, into the right perspective.

This is a game for any number of players. Whoever fields the ball can bowl – and take it in turn to bat. Don't forget to add up your runs.

Square Ball

This is a game for two players. A court about 12 feet by 12 feet is marked out and a line drawn across the centre. The players stand at opposite ends of the court, outside the square, and throw a ball so that it bounces in the section in front of their opponent. The aim is to get the ball past him, which scores a point for the thrower. The other player attempts to catch the ball and throw it back in the same manner. The best game can be played by using a large ball, such as a plastic football, which must be caught and returned, not punched.

A point is gained by the thrower every time he gets it past his opponent, or the opponent fails to catch it. The receiver gains a point if the ball does not bounce, or bounces twice, or bounces out of the side of the court instead of over the back line, or if the thrower throws from a side line instead of a back line.

Mini-Volleyball

This is a high-speed game that takes a lot of energy. The full volleyball game has as many rules as football but it is easily adaptable for a game on the beach, at camp, or on the lawn. A large lightweight plastic ball is required and a rope stretched tightly about 8 feet high and 15 feet long. This goes across the centre of the court which can be of any convenient size provided the side and back lines are marked clearly. Two teams of between two and six players make the best game and the aim is to hit the ball with the hands only and make it touch the ground in the opposing team's area. Scoring is like that for table tennis; the first team to score twenty-one points with a two-point clear majority. Service is taken from the right-hand corner close to the rope and then the ball is punched backwards and forwards over the rope until one team drops it. A point is claimed by the team which sent the ball over. Points are claimed for the opposing team if the ball goes out of their court without being touched by a player or touching the ground, or if the ball fails to clear the rope from the opposite team's punch and drops back to the ground. A point is also claimed if the ball fails to clear the rope on a serve. If the ball touches the rope on the way over during a serve, the serve must be taken again. If the same thing happens on the second serve, the serving team gives away a point. Players on the same side may punch-pass the ball to each other three times before sending it over the rope.

Hit the Bucket

You can have a lot of fun with a plastic bucket, the kind you find in the kitchen cupboard for kitchen use, not the seaside bucket-and-spade type. Put one in the back of the car sometime especially if it is a very hot day when you don't feel much like chasing around but still want to do something.

Hit the Bucket is a very simple game. Put the bucket down on the grass or sand with a heavy stone inside so that it won't get knocked over. You stand round it in a circle, at varying distances, according to the number of players available. Then you try and get a tennis ball or a golf ball into the bucket with a single throw.

It's not as easy as it sounds. Try a tennis ball first. Soak the ball if it is a very hot day to make it easier to handle. Probably with a little practice you can aim well and get the ball in the bucket first time. The secret is to try and hit the side of the bucket so that the ball will run round the sides and stay in.

A golf ball is much harder, especially if it hits the stone in the bottom of the bucket. But with patience and practice it can be done at varying distances. After one complete round with both tennis and golf balls, you stand another yard back and start again. And so on until you feel you've had enough. The winner is the boy or girl with the greatest number of successful throws.

If you have not got enough space for a circle you can still play it on a long pitch. Put the bucket at one end and stand on a line at varying distances from say 3 to 20 or more yards to make your throws.

Don't damage the bucket, whatever you do, and return it from whence it came when you get back home. Not very suitable for keeping in a games bag!

Floorball
This is one of the best games I know for winter evenings in a clubroom, but it can easily be adapted into a fine beach game for the family, or a game for the picnic outing.

Outdoors I like it best on a firm hard beach at low tide, the kind where you have a harbour wall or a stone or wooden groyne or a jetty or something like that. Then you can easily mark up a goal like the little goals they have in five-aside TV soccer games. You need one goalie to defend his goal.

The rest of you fire shots at him from all angles. You must shoot with hands only – *no kicking*. A soft ball – a fairly tough, large rubber ball, a beach ball or a light football are best for this game.

Each player must use only *one hand*. The game starts with one player in possession whose object is to fire a hard, low shot at the goal, and the goalie is the only person who can use both hands to stop it. The ball must never travel higher than one foot off the ground. Keep it on or near the ground. Encourage slick, feinting moves.

If there is a foul (kicking the ball, shooting higher than one foot, charging anyone in possession of the ball and any other local rules you wish to make) the game is re-started with a bounce-up. The most successful exponents of Floorball develop almost a rugby drop-kick effect by hitting the ball accurately and hard with the palm of the hand, so that it shoots low and straight at the goal as soon as the ball reaches them on the bounce. The goalie needs to be very alert.

Floorball is a great game for all boys but I have known many girls who like hockey and netball, and other sports, do very well at it on a breezy morning on the beach. Try it for yourself.

By the way, there is no need to log scores in this game unless you want to do so. Let everyone have a shot at being goalie. The one who lets in the most shots can buy everyone a Coke later.

Below Knee Ball

A game for six or more people. All players stand in a circle and then one or two go into the centre. The outside players throw a football at them and try to hit them below the knees. Any player hit leaves the centre and joins the other players on the outside circle and throws at the remaining players in the centre. Three players in the middle at a time makes a fast, lively game. Those in the middle may punch the ball away but if their hands touch the ball while below the level of their knees, they are out.

Barricade

A variation on Below Knee Ball. The playing area is divided into four equal parts by drawing lines across from side to side. Players are divided into two equal teams and face each other in the two centre sections. A football is tossed into the middle and whichever team secures it starts the game. The aim is to throw the ball at the opposing team and try to hit them below the knees. Any player hit goes into the section *behind* the opposing team and when the ball passes through the team he may pick it up and throw at the team in front of him. This means that the teams are attacked from the front and the rear. Except when the rear sections are vacant, at the beginning of the game, no player may cross a line and anyone who does so is out and goes behind the opposing team.

Malayan Football
This is a favourite game with Malayan children who use light balls woven in basketwork, but any ball of about 6 inches diameter upwards will do. Any number of players form a circle and attempt to keep the ball in the air by using their feet, knees, or head – no hands allowed. Count the number of times the ball is touched and try to improve the score every time. For the first few games the ball may be allowed to bounce once between each touch but after that it should not touch the ground.

Handball
This is a game with strict rules for which Leagues are organized all over Britain. Although basically an indoor game, it is great fun to play outdoors, particularly on short turf. There are two teams of six players, each defending a goal. The teams comprise a goalkeeper, two backs and three forwards. The ball must be played with the hands only along the ground, and each team attempts to score in the opposing goal. Only the goalkeepers are allowed to use two hands on the ball, all other players may only use one hand at a time. When a goalie gets two hands on the ball it is dead, even if he carries it back into the goal. Centres and goal kicks are taken, just as in football, and many of the same rules apply. A player may only be tackled if he has the ball, and the ball

may only be played if the player is on his feet. The goal-keeper must remain on his knees the *whole time*! No scooping of the ball is allowed by any player. The ball *must* be hit with the fist.

Kingy!

A favourite game with a small ball, particularly for a dozen players or more. The aim is for one player to throw the ball at the others and, when hit, they join the thrower until all are eliminated. A soft sorbo or tennis ball should be used and the playing area should be agreed beforehand; anyone running outside the playing area has to join the throwers.

The players stand in a circle on level ground and the ball is thrown straight up in the centre of the ring. Whoever's feet are *touched* first is 'Kingy' – the thrower. As soon as Kingy is touched by the ball he picks it up and counts loudly up to ten while the other players scatter as far as the playing area will allow. Then he throws the ball at them. A strict rule of the game is that no thrower may run with the ball: he must stand still as soon as he catches it. He can then throw it at one of the 'free' players, or, when he is joined by other throwers, pass it to another thrower. The free players can punch away the ball with a closed fist but if the ball touches any other part of their body they become throwers.

Tin Can Copper

A lively game for two teams with any number of equal players. All that is needed is a soft ball – tennis or sorbo – a can (or something of similar size) and three small stones. Teams are chosen and the toss is taken for Coppers and Robbers. Both teams stand in a circle round the can which has the three stones on it, balanced on top of each other. A Robber stands 10 feet from the can and has three throws with the ball, attempting to knock the stones off. If he does not succeed, another Robber has three shots, and so on until the whole team has tried. If nobody succeeds the other team becomes Robbers and try their hand.

As soon as a Robber knocks over the can both teams scatter, except for one Copper who becomes Warder. He gets the ball and throws it to another member of his team, or tries to hit a Robber. Any Robber hit drops out, temporarily. The aim of the game is for the Robbers to try and build up the can and stones again and for the Coppers to prevent them by hitting them with the ball and eliminating them.

The Warder guards the can – which he must not touch – and when a Robber attempts to set up the can and stones he calls for the ball to be thrown at the Robber. No Copper may run while holding the ball, or touch a Robber in any way. Robbers may punch away the ball with fists. When a Robber sets up the can, one point is claimed which is used to bring one of his number back into the game on the rule of first man out – first back in.

Change sides, after three points have been scored, or all the Robbers are eliminated.

Pass Ball

This has a number of variations from three players standing still to two teams on a playing field. The basic game is the old Pig in the Middle in which two players toss a ball to each other and a third player, between them, tries to intercept the ball either by catching it or picking it up if it is dropped. The player who *threw* the ball then becomes Pig and goes into the middle.

The first variation needs at least four players divided into two teams. The ball is simply passed between members of one team while the other team try to intercept it. The aim is simply to keep the ball as long as possible, and the only rules are: no running with the ball and no tackling of other players.

Now, with a few more players on each side, set up some form of target behind each team. They can be anything, such as two trees, two piles of coats, two deck-chairs, or anything similar and the aim is for each team to try and hit the target

behind the opposing side. If there are sufficient numbers on each side, one player can be a defender and in this case a large circle is drawn round the target into which no other player is allowed to step. The defender stands in the circle to fend off the ball from the target. For this game it is best if a ball of football size is used.

Another variation is for two teams to try to get the ball to their own goalkeeper. The same rules apply as the previous games – and the ones about running with the ball and tackling other players must be observed strictly or the game loses control – only this time the player in the circle is *behind* the opposing team and there is no target. The aim is for a team to pass the ball to their goalkeeper in the circle. If a goal is scored, the team it was scored against takes a throw-out from beside the goal. Free throws can be awarded against any team tackling or running with the ball and in the case of any dispute the ball is thrown high into the air between two players, who are the only ones allowed to touch it.

Cork and Ball

All that is needed is a small ball and a large cork, or small plastic tumbler. A piece of hard, level ground about a yard square has a circle marked on it about a yard in diameter and the cork placed in the centre. Two players stand some ten paces back from the circle on opposite sides and throw the ball at the cork, attempting to knock it out of the circle. The ball is caught by the player on the opposite side, who throws it back in the same way. The player who finally knocks the cork right out of the circle is the winner.

The game can be played by a number of players in pairs, each pair having a ball. All throw at the cork at the same time and the pair that knock the cork out are the winners.

Stone Ball

A circle a foot in diameter is drawn about 6 inches from a wall and three small stones placed inside it. Players stand at least 3 feet from the circle and throw a ball at the stones so that the ball bounces in the circle, rebounds off the wall and is caught by the player. The aim is to knock the stones right out of the circle in as few throws as possible. This game can be played by one player, who counts the throws taken and tries to improve his score each time, or by two players standing side by side and using just one ball (as the ball rebounds from a throw the other player catches it), or by two players having a ball each and using the same target, or by several players having a target each.

If two players use the same target, it is the player who knocks out the most stones who is the winner.

Line-Out

This is a fine simple outdoor game taken straight from Rugby Union football. It will help you to learn to jump properly and stretch your muscles; especially good on a breezy day when the wind might carry balls a good way and spoil many games. You need an empty rugby or soccer case (the outer leather part of the ball) stuffed lightly with old towels – don't make it too heavy. The idea is to get the feel of a ball without the bounce and liveliness of a ball with air in it.

Now the leader stands in front of a 'line' of players facing him, one behind the other. The first should be about 2 yards away – the others a yard behind each other or a little closer. Smallest players at the front of the queue, biggest and tallest at the back.

In addition to the leader, you need a 'scrum-half' who will stand on one side of him 2 or 3 yards back, roughly about the middle of the line. The aim of the game is to get possession of the ball and pass it out to the scrum-half.

The leader lobs the 'ball' gently with both hands over the heads of the players so that they have to jump and try to catch it with both hands, at the same time twisting or turning so that they pass it swiftly to the scrum-half wherever he or she is standing. The leader will vary his throws so that everybody is given a fair chance of jumping, catching and passing – but as you get into the fun of it the idea is to battle for possession.

If you get very good at it you can play with a real boy's size rugby ball on any beach or common. The scrum-half can vary his position on either side of the line-out or dodge about a bit to make the pass to him easier, or more difficult, according to the capabilities of the players.

If you are out for the day with friends and there are enough players, you can have a real competition line-out as in any game of rugby. Then the two lines stand side by side, mark each other, and try and pass the ball swiftly when possession is gained to the scrum-half. You need two scrum-halves if you have two lines of players, one on each side, and they can encourage their players with all sorts of cheerful shouts and suggestions!

7 TAG GAMES, BLINDFOLD GAMES AND RELAY RACES

TAG GAMES

Tag

This is probably one of the oldest games in the world and has various names – 'It', 'Touch', 'He', and so on. Basically, it is one player chasing others and whoever he touches becomes 'It'. The only rules are to keep to the area in which

the game is being played, and the 'no having back' rule, which means that when the chaser touches a player he cannot be touched back by the new chaser.

The game can be more fun if a few 'homes' are added – areas where players can rest but the chaser is not allowed in, but there must be a time limit on how long a player may rest. The fastest and funniest game of this type is called **Buzz** and the best way to play is in a fairly small area with some trees *but* there must be fewer trees, which are the 'homes', than players. In the garden, other objects can be used: the clothes-line post, garden shed, rockery, and so on.

The chaser has to touch another player in the usual way while those fortunate enough to find a home must touch it. There must only be one player to a home and as soon as another player runs to that home and says 'Buzz' the first player has to run away and find a new home, or be caught by the chaser. If he doesn't leave the home after being told to 'Buzz', he can be touched by the chaser.

In **Add-on Tag**, any player touched by the chaser also starts to chase until in the end, the whole 'team' are chasers and the last player touched is the winner.

In **Chain Tag** the same rules apply but this time the chasers must link hands and form a chain to chase the remaining players.

If the area is small, like a garden, a good variation is for the players being chased to be in their own 'home' by, for example, standing on one leg holding their left foot in the right hand and their right ear with their left hand! While a player stands like that he cannot be touched but as soon as he puts a foot down, or releases his ear, the chaser may touch him!

If there are sufficient players for two teams of at least six a side, then **Release** is a favourite variation of Tag. It needs a fairly large area, like a park or, better still, a wood. One team scatters over the area while the other team, the chasers, choose a base. This can be a tree, or large bush, or anything similar. The chasers attempt to capture the free team by tapping any player gently (!) on the head three times and then bringing him back to the base. The free team then have to try and release any caught players by touching them.

Some rules have to be observed here otherwise the game can be spoiled. A player is caught when he is tapped on the head three times, even if he has his hands on his head; a captured player may not be released until he is at the base; and a captured player must be actually touching part of the base before he can be released by his team. Change sides after an agreed time, or if all the free team get captured.

Another variation for a larger group is **Flag Raiding**. Attempts are made to capture other players but each team also has a flag, or something similar, in their bases and these can be captured by the rival team. The first team to capture a flag can be the winner, or the flag can be bartered back for, say, two prisoners.

Crossover Tag
One player is 'It' in the usual way and chases the others but when another player crosses between them the chaser must immediately chase the second player, even if the crossing is accidental. A touched player becomes 'It' and continues the game.

Hide and Seek
One of the oldest and most popular of all children's games. One player hides his eyes and counts slowly and loudly to twenty while the others run and hide. At the end of the count the chaser goes to look for them and touches anyone he can find. In the meantime, the players must try to get home without being touched. Last player touched becomes the chaser and the game starts again. Now for some variations:

Hi-You!
Played the same as Hide and Seek but when the chaser finds a player he must identify him, call out his name loudly and then both of them race back to the home. If the chaser

reaches the home first, the other player must join him in searching for the remainder; if the other player reaches home first, the chaser must continue searching by himself. Last player found becomes chaser.

Sardines

This is an indoor game that is great fun outdoors provided it is played in an area with plenty of cover. All the players except one cover their eyes and the one player goes off and hides. After counting to thirty, the remaining players scatter and search for the first one and as each one finds him they join him in his hiding place, as quietly as possible. If the first player has been clever, he will have chosen a place that will hide only about half the players comfortably – and that's where the sardine part comes in! The last player to discover the rest then goes off to hide.

Throw Tag

A home line is marked out at one end of the games area and a starting line at the other. On the centre of the starting line a bucket is placed, or a circle is drawn in the sand or on the ground, and all the players except one stand on the starting line, keeping as far from the bucket as they can. The remaining player stands 10 feet from the bucket and tries to toss a ball or pebble into it. If he does not succeed, nothing happens and he recovers the ball or picks up another pebble. If the ball goes into the bucket and stays there, all the players make a rush for the home line and the thrower tries to touch one. The first player touched becomes the thrower. The thrower does not have to recover the ball before chasing the players.

BLINDFOLD GAMES

Blind Man's Buff

The oldest blindfold game of them all. One player is blindfolded, spun round a few times then set loose to try and

locate the other players. There are two methods of playing:
the first is when the Blind Man touches another player and
that player becomes the Blind Man; the second is where the
Blind Man catches a player and tries to identify him by
feeling his face or clothes. If he succeeds, the caught player
becomes the Blind Man; if he fails he carries on as
catcher.

String Trail

This is fun for players and spectators if the trail is laid out
sensibly. A long piece of string is led round the garden or
games area, under bushes, over logs, round trees or sheds.
Its height can vary between a few inches above the ground to
over head height. Three or four players are blindfolded carefully and have to follow the trail by touching the string with
their fingers. They can either play as one or more teams, or
individually. The game should be played on a time basis
with the player completing the course and following the
string the closest as the winner.

Blind Guide

This is for two or more teams and every player, except two
team leaders, is blindfolded. A course is marked out for
each team consisting of a number of obstacles around which
the teams have to walk. The leader stands at the rear of the
team and each player places his hands on the shoulders of
the man in front. No talking is allowed and the object is for
the leader to guide his team round the obstacles up to a
marker at the end of the course and then round the obstacles
again and back to their place. He does this by simply press-
ing on the shoulders of the man in front of him, who repeats
the signal down the line until the player at the front receives
it and leads the line accordingly. The signals are simple: a
tap with the right hand means 'turn right'; tap left hand –
turn left; both hands together – stop; tap in the centre of the
back – move backwards. The teams move off one after the

other on a signal from an umpire. Give as many points as there are obstacles, including the end-of-course marker, and deduct a point for each obstacle missed or knocked over.

Blindfold Cudgels
A game that is great fun for onlookers as well as players. Two players are blindfolded and each is given a rolled news-paper and a small bell. The spectators form a ring and the two players creep round in it, ringing their bells and trying to hit each other with the paper cudgels. There is no winner – the game is just for fun!

Blindfold Boxing
This is the same as the Cudgels game except that the two players wear boy's boxing-gloves and do not carry bells. A good referee is necessary!

Blind King
One player is blindfolded and sits at one end of the games area with the remainder at the other end. The area between them is strewn with small twigs and branches, anything that will make a noise if touched. Players take it in turn to try and creep up on the King and touch him. An umpire stands behind the King who points to any noise he hears. If the umpire decides the King is pointing at a moving player, that player is out and he must sit down at the spot where he was caught.

TEAM GAMES

There are a number of games that can be played by two teams in which individual players from each team oppose each other. Players should be divided equally so that there are members of equal weight and size in each team. Give each player a number, starting with one for the tallest, and so on, down the line and then line the two teams up facing each other with the tallest player in each team facing the smallest in the other. This is because many of these games require equipment that is placed centrally between the lines and so when the players' numbers are called they run from opposite ends of their teams and do not get in each other's way. Players may sit on the ground until their number is called.

Hopping Charge
A number is called and the two players with that number hop towards each other with their arms folded and try to knock each other off balance. Make sure that shoulders are used for charging, not elbows. If the two players take rather a long time to finish the game, the umpire can bring on two other players at the same time. The players must continue to hop on the same foot until the umpire calls 'Change'.

Dog and Bone
This is another hopping game only players do not have to be knocked off-balance. A cap, scarf, handkerchief or something similar is placed in the centre between the two lines and when their number is called the players hop to the centre. The object is to get the 'bone' back to their place without being touched. It is a game of bluff with both players making mock snatches at the bone until one of them really does pick it up and makes a wild hop back to his place before he can be touched. A player loses the game if he puts a foot down.

Stick and Ball
For this game two thick sticks about 12 inches long are required, together with a ball, any size will do but a small football is best. A garden chair or stool is placed between the ends of the teams and the ball is placed in the centre, between the teams, with a stick on each side. The teams are called A and B, and each chair is labelled in the same way.

When their numbers are called the two players run out, pick up the stick nearest them and attempt to bat the ball between the legs of the chair. The ball may go under the chair from any angle to count as a goal.

Two-man Handball
This is played exactly as Stick and Ball except the hands are used instead of sticks. Only one hand may touch the ball at a time.

Hot Seat
Three chairs or stools are needed for this game. Two are placed either end of the playing area and one in the centre. The two end chairs are labelled A and B and two teams are given the same letters. Each team member is given a number. When the players' numbers are called they have to run round the chair with their team's letter on it and try to be first to sit on the centre chair. Some players will be nearer their team's chair than others and so will have less distance to run; when every player has had at least one turn, change the letters on the chairs to the opposite ends so that the distance is increased for those players.

RELAY RACES

There are many variations on the simple relay race and new ones can be invented, according to where the races are to be run. To make a relay contest enjoyable, two teams with not less than four players are required. Be sure that everybody knows the rules – which should be as few as possible – before the races start. It is a good idea to have some form of baton for handing over – a small stick or even a handkerchief will do – and if a course is used where the runner runs up to the end and back to his team, each player should have to go to the rear end of his team on the way back, round the back of the team and then up to the front to hand over the baton. This stops any runners starting off before their time.

The basic relay race is where the first runner races to the end of the course, runs back and touches the next man, and then goes to the end of the team, and so on. Simple variations are running up and hopping back, or running backwards, or hopping backwards, or a combination of any of them. Here are some other variations:

Chain Race
The first man runs up the course and back, goes behind the team and back to his place, where the second runner holds him round the waist or by the belt and they both run up the course and back and pick up the third runner. Carry on until the whole team is running, then on the next leg the leader drops out into his original place, on the following leg the second runner drops out, and so on, until the whole team are back in place.

Agility Relay
This is a really exhausting one! The players run up and down a course in the usual manner but the fun is that when a player is running, all the rest of the team are doing something also, and complete chaos will result if it is not done properly! Each player runs up the course and back to his team; as he does so the team sit on the ground and stretch their legs out to the left. The runner has to jump over the team on his way to the rear. The moment he reaches the end, the team swing round so that their legs are out to the *right*; the runner must jump over them and race up to the end of the course again. As he comes back the team jump to their feet and open their legs, making a tunnel for him to crawl through. As soon as he is at the back they all crouch down so that he comes over their backs and back to his place, when the second man goes off on the same sequence. One thing to remember is that all the players, apart from the

leader, must go over the backs of any players in front of him when starting off and finishing his run.

Silverstone Relay

For any number of teams with an equal number of players in each. The teams stand in single file like the spokes of a wheel, with the leader at the rim and the last men, backs to each other, at the hub. In front of each leader are two garden chairs, sticks or anything similar, even a pile of coats, about a yard apart. These are the entrances to the pits and every player must pass in and out of them. On the starting signal the leaders race out of the pits and run left round the circle and back into their own pits, then the second man takes up the race, and so on. When the last man has run, the whole team run together on a 'lap of honour' behind their leader and back into their pits. First team back in position is the winner. No pushing of other runners is allowed and any player who touches the entrance to any pit, even his own team's, must return and start again.

Fire, Fire!

Not all relays have to be run at breakneck speed. This race calls for a steady hand and a long sit down! Teams are arranged like the spokes of a wheel with the leaders facing each other in the centre and their teams in file behind them. All are seated on the ground and the leaders have a bucket of water between them and each holds a teaspoon. The last player in each team has a cup on the ground in front of him and the object is for the leader to take a spoonful of water and pass it to the player behind him. The spoon is passed down the line to the last man who tips the water into the cup and passes the spoon back for another filling. The game must be run to a strict time limit, about two minutes is enough, and then each team's cup of water measured carefully to find the winner. Players must sit facing forward all the time and may only turn from the waist.

Tunnel Ball

A game for any number of teams with an equal number of players, but more fun for two large teams rather than several small ones. Each team has a ball, football size preferably, but any ball will do. On the starting signal the teams jump feet astride and the leader rolls the ball through his legs and players pass it on through their legs until it reaches the last man, who picks it up and runs to the front and repeats the process, the whole team moving backwards one place each time.

Over Ball

This is played just like Tunnel Ball but instead the ball, or any other object, such as a walking stick, umbrella, spade or bucket, is passed backwards over each player's head to the last man.

8 OBSERVATION GAMES

Not all games need to be of the running-around type, or need skill with the hands or feet. Skill with the eyes is equally important and very satisfying. Using one's eyes for games can be fun.

Scavenger Hunt
A list of items to collect, or objects to be discovered and recorded, or information to be gathered, is given to each player. A time limit is set and points are given for each item found. The time limit must be strictly adhered to, and it is a good idea to give two points for each object so that if the item discovered is not quite what was wanted only one point is awarded.

Suggestions for items: a stone with a hole in it; the leaves from five different trees, which must be named correctly; an empty case from a ball-point pen; a woodpigeon's feather; a card from a tea packet featuring a ship (or whatever is in current vogue), and so on. The list should be varied to suit the surroundings so that a game in town would be different from one in the country.

Scavenging for information is usually better for games in and near a town park, but the umpire (ie, the leader) must know the answers beforehand. Suggested items: the time the last bus leaves the station (public parks are often very near to stations); the telephone number of the call-box at the corner of the High Street; the name of the house with the red door in Broad Close, and so on.

First Seen

This game can be played by any number of players on some form of journey: rambling, train ride, coach trip, or even a car journey, provided that the driver is not involved. A list is prepared beforehand of items to look for and the first player to see any one of them shouts out and scores a point. The list must be prepared according to the type of journey. It is no use trying to spot a robin or a bee from a moving train or car! A church with a steeple, or a tower, or a bridge over a river, are more the things for this type of journey. Remember that the umpire must see them as well. For a country walk, smaller objects or ones less easily seen may be listed, such as wild flowers, or a pheasant, or a certain type of car registration, once again depending upon the area.

Spotters

This is a good game for town or for a car journey. A list of less usual cars, or dogs, is made up and the first player to spot anything on the list claims a point. It is not just the *first* time seen that a point is claimed but *each* time the object is seen. It is sometimes more fun to have two lists; cars for the boys, and dogs, for example, for the girls. The game can also be played on a walk in the country, using trees, birds, flowers, or even types of farm machinery.

Rice Trail

Tracking is always fun and demands a keen eye but if a trail is laid by one player for the rest to follow it becomes much more of a game. One of the best ideas is to use rice or mixed chicken corn because it does not look untidy and wild birds and animals are glad to have it. Do not use chalk or paper because both of these spoil the look of town and country. Rice can be used in town, as well, but it must be agreed beforehand at what part of the road it will be dropped: in the right-hand gutter, for example, and then nobody will have to continually cross the road to search for the trail. Little rice need be used, just a sprinkling every so often on a long path. Where there are cross-paths or junctions the rice should be sprinkled immediately at the entrance to the path taken or immediately after the junction if the trail layer is continuing on the main path.

Bird Watching

Few outdoor activities can give more lasting fun and pleasure over the years than watching wild birds and animals. You will find many opportunities for watching wild birds and recording what you see and hear in parks, on country walks, on wide expanses of open common and woodland, moorland and along our varied and immensely interesting coastline in Britain.

Young people with their sharp eyes and keen ears often make extremely good bird watchers and, before long, learn to distinguish all the finches, predators, waders and seabirds, as well as the many common British birds found in gardens at all seasons of the year. Very little equipment is needed and the most important is a simple diary-notebook; it is essential to note down what is seen and when, ie, the time of day, what the birds are eating or doing, and so on.

More and more research needs to be done on the feeding habits of birds, and their roosting sites. Far too little is known about the distribution of British birds and the local migration of birds, which may only be a mile or two. Often this is connected with food supplies at certain seasons of the year, but sometimes it has no apparent significance at all and is puzzling.

Perhaps birds like a change of scenery just as much as human beings. Perhaps they react to a sudden change in the direction of a prevailing wind. There are so many fascinating problems and they greatly interest alert, lively young minds. To the notebook and pencil you need only add a pair of binoculars and a sound, modern bird reference book to have all the equipment you need.

The Royal Society for the Protection of Birds, Sandy, Bedfordshire, has a special section for Junior Bird Recorders, and projects are constantly in progress; these give ideas for family outings and with them a good deal of family fun. It is really a continuous outdoor game in which parents and young people can take part. It starts in gardens and parks, continues with picnics and treks of all kinds, and may well end up as a prime reason for the choice of the place for family holidays!

Journeys

Boredom on *car journeys* seems to be a problem for many families, especially when they get held up in traffic queues and jams. Perhaps the parents are more bored than the children sometimes. The successful 'I Spy' games are based on Observation and often fill up the odd twenty minutes. 'First . . .' is an obvious one here. First to see a yellow Labrador dog, a black spaniel, a white poodle, and so on. First to see a policeman with a flat cap, a helmet, a moustache, a beard, a bicycle . . . First to see a fire engine, a baker's van, a milk float, a telephone engineer's van, a post office van and so on.

Or a lady in a white hat, a green coat, a boy with red hair, a girl in pigtails, a man with a walking stick . . . all the everyday life of the street.

In the country, attention is easily drawn to the animals in the fields. We may have some particular 'friends' such as a brown-and-white cow, a black-and-white cow (do not specify the breed – it is fatal!) a white pig, a black sheep, a red pony, a goat, a donkey . . . when the particular friend is seen and spotted *'Friend!'* rends the air, but not so loudly it alarms the lady driving the car ahead. If, in fact, it is not a 'friend' at all the cry of *'No! Foe!'* is heard and the culprit must pay a forfeit. Children love forfeits and it is worth spending a little time working out a few choice ones which will make everybody smile, including the recipient.

Boredom during *train journeys* can be counteracted with a sketching block and a bold, black pencil or crayon. First person draws a face and the rest have to add to it in turn until a completely dressed figure results. This game always takes up loads of time, thank goodness! I have a friend who entertains his children on trains with a small theatrical box containing one or two false moustaches, spectacle frames, false and quite alarming noses, a black eye patch, and so on. The use of these dispels any tendency to boredom, even if it is not quite understood by visitors from overseas spending a holiday in Britain. It would be as well to use some discretion with the false noses at important stops.

9 GAMES FOR YOUNGER BROTHERS AND SISTERS

Finally, here are a few games especially for younger brothers and sisters. They can, of course, join in most of the other games in the book, but you will be very popular with Mum if you know one or two games that are especially suitable for youngsters.

Wolf
This is a very good game for younger children who are in, or just out of, the nursery-rhyme stage. All you need is a

mat – a slip mat will do, or a car mat, or anything similar. Place it in a corner of the grassy glade where you are having your picnic, or a sand-dune or anywhere similar.

Someone has to be Wolf. It could be Dad or an older brother or sister. Wolf retires to his or her den, which is the mat. He lies on it apparently fast asleep.

The children can approach stealthily or crawl up to the Wolf and around him to have a good look at him, fast asleep. This can go on for some time.

But soon Wolf shows signs of waking up! He yawns, stretches his arms and legs, turns over, grunts and makes strange wolf-like noises. (Very strange, I must say, sometimes.) When Wolf wakes up he is very hungry, naturally, and what makes a better meal than a boy or girl? As soon as Wolf utters all these warning sounds, the children must scatter and hide and have to be very quiet indeed. Wolf must not find them.

But, of course, Wolf may not be so hungry after all and decides to curl up on his mat again and have some more sleep. The children reappear, thinking the coast is clear, and pop along again to have a good look at him, crawling around on all fours.

At last Wolf *is* hungry. He yawns, half-opens his eyes, shuts them again, scratches himself and stretches his legs – for the purpose of this game he has four, of course. The children have scattered far and wide, under bushes, behind trees, rocks and hedges, even a little way up a tree, perhaps, or under a groundsheet. Not a child in sight, in fact!

Wolf sniffs the air and starts hunting on all fours. He sniffs the ground and prowls around in search of prey. He may be lucky. He may not be so lucky. As soon as he catches something for dinner he has to get it back (on all fours) to his den (the mat). But the other children naturally prevent such a disaster. The game ends when Wolf has caught, and successfully carried back to his den, all the players. Great fun for all concerned!

Crabs

Crabs is a good game for the little 'uns and it is ideal for the beach or picnic spot. Youngsters up to about six years or so enjoy it immensely. You should be wearing plimsolls (or pumps) or sandals or be barefoot.

The little boy or girl stands on your feet facing you and holding on to you by hands and arms. There should be a good space between you – not a bear hug!

Then, with a swaying, rocking motion very like a seaside crab, you walk slowly forward taking the youngster with you on your feet. To the spectator it looks just like a crab, the young boy or girl moving backwards most of the time on your feet; but sometimes you reverse and then the youngster takes control for a time.

I have seen people walk quite a long way with younger brothers and sisters playing Crabs. Of course, it's really a ride for them too, but it is surprising how much confidence it can instil in a young boy or girl who is perhaps afraid of moving backwards.

The Badger

This is good fun for young children but I have known people of all ages to get a lot of fun and enjoyment out of it. You need to make a 'badger' which can be an old cushion which has seen its best days, or an old pillowslip filled with straw or crumpled-up newspapers, or anything else suitable.

The 'badger' is tied on to a long rope – about 10 to 12 feet is ideal and something that makes a noise is also tied on the 'badger' at the point where the rope is tied. This could be a small bag containing coins, keys or pebbles, or a small tin money-box with a few coins in it, or a tinkling little bell – the kind you put on a cat's collar if it shows any signs of wanting to catch birds. Anything that tinkles or makes a pleasant, easily recognizable little noise is sufficient.

Now one or two little boys and girls are blindfolded and

have to get down on all fours on the grass or beach. Just make sure before you play a game like this that there are no bits of glass or rough stones about.

The blindfolded youngsters have to catch the 'badger' as soon as the game starts. Dad or an older brother or sister is in charge of the game and has to pull or drag the 'badger' skilfully among the catchers so that they don't grab it. The little bell or noise of the coins or pebbles gives its position away at once.

Before long you will attract other boys and girls who want to play but Dad is going to have a hard time of it if there are more than three or four at a time.

You will all enjoy yourselves immensely playing The Badger, especially Mum and any other spectators. They can ensure that no boy or girl strays outside the little area or circle chosen for the game.

Remember, you must be on all fours except Dad, who can dodge about with the 'badger' as much as he likes so long as he always keeps it on the deck. Good blindfolds, too, please. No peeping or you pay a forfeit.

The Pattern Game (also called **Shapes**)
The Pattern Game often keeps young children happy for a long time – it is a good game for those sticky days in the summer when no one feels much like racing or chasing about. You can play it almost anywhere outdoors and it is a group game in the sense that you can't very well play it unless you have several children. About four or five is an ideal number.

Mum or Dad has to dream up a pattern or shape. This can be a geometric pattern such as a circle, square, triangle, rectangle – anything the children will recognize easily and quickly. We can forget all about octagons, hectagons, and so on, for this game!

Other patterns or shapes would include the half-moon or crescent, letters of the the alphabet, numbers including those with two or three digits such as 77 or 111.

As soon as a shape is called out, the children rush to form it lying on the ground, if necessary head to toe, and so on. They soon get the hang of it and become astonishingly clever at making themselves into, say, a number 5 with the use of arms and legs and hair.

Jumbo

A popular game for the under-fives but one in which anyone can join for the fun of the family game. A large circle – but not too large – is drawn on the sand with a stick or dibber, or can be roughly marked out on grass with headscarfs, hankies or the white plastic clothes-line from the games bag.

Each person, in turn, is Jumbo, and has to proceed at his or her own pace on all fours like an Indian elephant round the circle with a load on his back. This load can be two or three books in a cardboard box, a basket of conkers, a carrier bag containing plimsolls, in fact, *anything*.

If the load comes off, he or she must start again and if the load comes off a second time he is out. The wise Jumbos take their time despite catcalling, howls of derision, shouts of encouragement, and so on, according to your family status, and I have known intense groans of disappointment rend the air when Dad won.

A trick of the trade is to carry the load high up on your back almost between your shoulder-blades rather than in the middle of the back.

All very simple, but good fun. When two or more people have completed the circle run, have a play-off until you get a winner.

Blow Football

This game needs a bit of preparation. The pitch is a rectangular, flat, folding board, ideally, but it can be improvised from carton packaging material; a very good alternative is a piece of hardboard or any similar material from the do-it-yourself shop. This can be cut so that it fits

the bottom of the car boot, or as you wish. Mark out a
football pitch with a felt pen on the hardboard, including the
place for the goals. It makes a better game if you have two
sets of goalposts with nets which you can make yourself or
buy at any good toy shop. Or they can be improvised with
plastic salt and pepper pots, matchboxes or anything which
will stand up on the board.

The ball is a table-tennis ball and the two players lie flat
on their tummies or crouch as low as they can while trying
to blow the ball through their opponent's goal. Boys will
play it for hours!

Granny's Footsteps (Ware, Wolf! in USA)

Grandmother's Footsteps, Grandma's Seen You!, Granny's
Footsteps, Ware, Wolf: (USA) and similar titles all refer to
the same game, which is a party game that can be played
almost anywhere with any number of people. It is *much
harder* to play outdoors because of the grass and sand, the
hum of a passing aeroplane or car or motorbike, the drone
of farm equipment, a barking dog, the noise of farm animals
or just the wind in the trees. It is a good test of hearing
anywhere.

One boy or girl who is Granny stands with his or her back
to the others at a distance of, say, 25 yards or what you can
manage. It spoils it to have less, I think. Each boy and girl
then moves slowly and stealthily towards Granny who starts
counting slowly and quietly at the word 'Go!'

She or he turns quickly at any number selected in advance, say fifteen, and if any person is caught moving they
are out and must sit down. The others carry on and Granny
starts counting again – the first boy or girl to touch Granny
on the back wins the ice-cream prize.

But when you play this game outdoors do try and select a
reasonably quiet place for it. If the odds are stacked too
heavily against Granny, then reduce her counting time to
anything you like say five, eight or ten.

TYPES OF GAMES

The number in brackets after the name of the game refers to the recommended number of players. Where no number is given the game is suitable for any number of players. The alphabetical index that follows will give you the page reference.

QUIET GAMES

Acorn Games
Bar Skittles
Bargain Hunting
Beach Golf
Bird Watching
  (activity)
Blind Pirates
Blow Football
Bowl of Stones
  (activity)
Circle Conkers
Conker Century
Conker Patterns
Crabs
Fetch
First Seen
Fly Casting
Granny's Footsteps
Kim's Compass
Lawn Golf
Nature Paintings
Nature Pictures
Outdoor Kim
Rings and Lobs
Sand Castles
Skimming
Spincatcher
Spotters
Tree Kim

Uncle Frank
Wild Flower Kim
Wild Grass Kim
Wolf
Write a Line

ACTIVE GAMES

Aeroplates
Apple Bobbing
Archery
The Badger
Beach Ball
Beach Sports Day
Blind Man's Buff
Blindfold Games
Bucket Corko [5–6]
Catch as Catch Can [2–4]
Catchstone
Conker Batman
Corko!
Courier
Dad's Only Race
Discus
Dog in Manger
Elements
Fire, Fire!
Flying Saucers
Freeze
French Bowls
French Cricket
Hide and Seek

High Jump
Hit the Bucket
Hi-You!
Hop, Skip and Jump
Hopscotch
Horseshoes
Human Chair
Jumbo
Long Jump
Mersey Tunnel
Mini-Olympics
Mum's Only Race
'Murps' (Marbles)
Orange Rolling
Patball [2]
Poison Pool
Pétanque
Putting the Shot
Rice Trail
Sardines
Scavenger Hunt
Skittles
Slap the Slipper
Sports Day (Mini-Olympics)
Statues
Throwing a Cricket Ball
Throwing the Football
Throwing the Hammer
Throwing the Javelin
Time Hop
Treasure Hunts
Tree Ball

LIVELY GAMES

Ankle Grab [2]
Ankle Tapping [2]
Beach Cricket
Beach Rounders
Beach Tennis [2–4]
Bucket Cricket
Bull's Eye
Buster [2–8]
Chariot Race
Chase the Thimble
Chinese Cymbals [2]

Chinese Wrestling [2]
Cork and Ball
Couples
Dog and Bone
Fill the Bucket
Grab!
Hoop Wrestling [2]
Hopping Charge
Horse Tally-ho
Heave-ho!
Hopping Charge
Hot Potato
Hot Seat
Indian Leg Wrestling
Jokari [1–2]
Jump the Rope
Kingy!
Line-Out
Magic Carpets [3–6]
Malayan Football
Mini-Olympics
Over Ball
Over My Shoulder [2]
Pass Ball
Pull Down
Push o' War
Quarter Staffs [2]
Rats and Rabbits
Rat Race
Release
Rowing
Run and Mount
Show Jumping
Smash and Grab
Sports Day Races
Sprint Tug o' War
Square Ball [2]
Square Hop [2–5]
Stick and Ball
Stone Ball
All Tag Games
Tail Tag [2]
Tin Can Copper
Top Dog [2]
Triangle Tug o' War [3]
Trust [6]

Tunnel Ball
Two-man Handball [2]
Twos and Threes
Wristo!

FAST GAMES

Barricade
Below Knee Ball
Chariot Race
Circle Ball
Floorball
Handball
Hot Rice (Version 1)

Hot Rice (Version 2)
Mini-Volleyball
Silverstone Relay

BOISTEROUS–GAMES

Agility Relay
Foul-Play Race
Horse Feathers
In and Out
Pandemonium
Squirters
Tailor's Dummy [3]

INDEX

Acorn Games, 54
Add-on Tag, 96
Aeroplates, 39–41
Agility Relay, 103–4
Ankle Grab, 66
Ankle Tapping, 65
Apple Bobbing, 54–5
Archery, 58

Badger, The, 115–16
Bag, Games, 9–11
Ball, Beach, 27
Ball Games, 81–94
Bar Skittles, 37
Bargain Hunting, 48–49
Barricade, 88–9
Beach Ball, 27
Beach Cricket, 21–2
Beach Games, 13–31
Beach Golf, 81–2
Beach Rounders, 16–17
Beach Sports Day, 29–31
Beach Tennis, 22–3
Below Knee Ball, 88
Bird Watching, 109–10
Blindfold Boxing, 100
Blindfold Cudgels, 100
Blindfold Games, 98–100
Blind Guide, 99–100
Blind King, 100

Blind Man's Buff, 98–9
Blind Pirates, 50–51
Blow Football, 117–18
Bottles, Plastic, 36
Boules, Les, 24–5
Bowl of Stones, 26
Bowls, French, 24–5
Bucket Corko, 18
Bucket Cricket, 75
Bull's Eye, 74–5
Buster, 65
Buzz, 96

Car Journeys, 110–11
Catch as Catch Can, 82–3
Catch Stone, 16
Chain Race, 103
Chain Tag, 96
Chariot Race, 29
Chase the Thimble, 72
Chinese Boxing, 64
Chinese Wrestling, 64
Circle Ball, 83–4
Circle Games, 71–9
Clothes Line, Plastic, 11
Conker Batman, 51–2
Conker Century, 51
Conker Patterns, 52
Conkers, 49–54
Cork and Ball, 93

Corko!, 17–18
Couples, 67–8
Courier, 39
Crabs, 115
Cricket, Beach, 21–2
Crossover Tag, 97

Dad's Only Race, 31
Discus, 56
Dog and Bone, 101
Dog in Manger, 76–7

Elements, 41
Exploring, Beach, 31

Fetch, 19
Figure-of-Eight Knot, 49
Fill the Bucket, 38
Fire, Fire!, 104
First Seen, 108
Flag Raiding, 97
Floorball, 87–8
Fly Casting, 45–6
Flying Saucers, 39–41
Forfeits, 18, 74, 75, 116
Foul-Play Race, 58
Four-legged Race, 57
Freeze, 14–15
French Bowls, 24–5
French Cricket, 84–5
'Frisby' Discus, 41

Games Bag, 9–11
Games Bag Tag, 10
*Games for Younger Brothers
    and Sisters*, 113–18

Games of Strength, 61–9
'*Getaway*' *Discus*, 41
Grab!, 52–3
Granny's Footsteps, 118

Handball, 89–90
Handball, Two-man, 102
Heave-Ho!, 65
Hi-You!, 97–8
Hide and Seek, 97
High Jump, 56–7
Hit the Bucket, 86–7
Hoop Wrestling, 65
Hop, Skip and Jump, 31
Hopping Charge, 101
Hopscotch, 15
Horse and Rider Games,
    67–9
Horse Feathers, 58–9
Horseshoes, 23–4
Horse Tally-ho!, 68
Hot Potato, 52
Hot Rice (1), 75–6
Hot Rice (2), 76
Hot Seat, 102
Human Chair, 72

I-Spy games, 110–11
In and Out, 19–20
Indian Leg Wrestling, 65

Javelin, 55–6
Jokari, 26–7
Jumbo, 117
Jump the Rope, 73

Kim, 43–5, 78–9
Kim's Compass, 78–9
Kingy!, 90

Lawn Golf, 81–2
Les Boules, 24
Line-out, 93–4
Litter Prevention, 53–4
Lobs, Rings and, 41–3
Long Jump, 31, 56

Magic Carpets, 16
Malayan Football, 89
Marbles, 46–7
Mersey Tunnel, 77–8
Mini-Olympics, 55–9
Mini-Volley ball, 85–6
Mums' Only Race, 31
'Murps', 46–7

Nature Paintings, 35
Nature Pictures, 35

Observation Games, 107–11
Orange Rolling, 36
Outdoor Kim, 43–4
Over My Shoulder, 62
Over Ball, 105
Overhand Knot, 49

Pandemonium, 48
*Parks and Gardens,
  Games for*, 33–59
Pass Ball, 91–3
Patball, 83
Pattern Game, The, 116–17

Pétanque, 24–5
Plastic Clothes Line, 11
Plate Spinning, 39–40
Poison Pool, 73
Pull Down, 67
Push o' War, 66
Putting the Shot, 56

Quarter Staffs, 61–2
Quoits, Outdoor, 23–4

Rat Race, 69
Rats and Rabbits, 68–9
Relay Races, 102–5
Release Tag, 96
Rice Trail, 109
Rings and Lobs, 41–3
*Round Turn and Two
  Half-Hitches Knot*, 54–5
Rounders, Beach, 16–17
Rowing, 58
Run and Mount, 68

Sand Castles, 13–14
Sardines, 98
Scavenger Hunt, 107–8
Shapes, 116–17
Show Jumping, 57
Silverstone Relay, 104
Skimming, 20–21
Skittles, 37
Slap the Slipper, 72
Smash and Grab, 75
Spincatcher, 74
Spotters, 108–9

Sprint Tug o War, 62
Square Ball, 85
Square Hop, 27–8
Squirters, 38
Statues, 14
Stick and Ball, 101–2
Stone Ball, 93
String Trail, 99

Tag, 95–8
Tag Games, 95–8
Tag, Games Bag, 10
Tail Tag, 66
Tailor's Dummy, 14
Team Games, 100–102
Tennis, Beach, 22–3
Throw Tag, 98
Throwing the Cricket Ball, 29
Throwing a Football, 30
Throwing the Hammer, 31
Throwing the Javelin, 30–31

Time Hop, 28–9
Tin Can Copper, 90–91
Top Dog, 63–4
Train Journeys, 111
Treasure Hunts, 33–5
Tree Ball, 72–3
Tree Kim, 45
Triangle Tug o' War, 66
Trust, 62–3
Trust Your Weight, 62–3
Tunnel Ball, 105
Two-man Hand Ball, 102
Twos and Threes, 71

Uncle Frank, 19

Ware, Wolf!, 118
Water Relay, 31
Wild Flower Kim, 44–5
Wild Grass Kim, 45
Wolf, 113–14
Wristo!, 64
Write a Line, 47–8

More fun with Piccolo

Alvin Schwartz
Tomfoolery 30p

Tricks with words to trip you up and muddle your friends.

Witcracks 30p
Jokes of all sorts: riddles, puns, ancient jokes, modern jokes,
shaggy dog stories, even 'Confucius say' jokes.

Piccolo Book of Jokes 20p
Margaret Gossett

Q. When is an operation funny?
A. When it leaves the patient in stitches.
There's a groan a minute in this collection of jokes, puns and
riddles.

Piccolo Book of Riddles 20p
S. B. Cunningham

A bumper book of riddles from around the world. All the old
chestnuts are included as well as a lot of new ones.

Denys Parsons
Fun-tastic! 25p
Even More Fun-tastic! 20p

Two collections of newspaper misprints and howlers, specially
selected for children.

Non-fiction

Everyday Inventions 35p
Meredith Hooper

From Coca Cola and the zip to the sewing machine and
television, nearly everything we use has been invented by someone
somewhere . . .

First Feats 25p
Peter Tunstall

Lindberg, Hillary, Magellan, Bell, Leonov – these men all
achieved a 'first' in their chosen field. Fifty exciting stories are told
in this lively anthology.

Piccolo Book of Amazing Scientific Facts 25p
Jane Sherman

Do you know . . .
That there is a metal which will melt in your hand?
How a camel stores water inside his body?
What is the fastest-moving creature in the world?
What makes a cobra dance?
Answers to these and many other amazing scientific facts are
given in this fascinating book.